CONFESSIONS OF A CHARISMATIC CHRISTIAN

Rick Dewhurst

Quotidian Books

Q

quotidian

ISBD: 978-1-7775730-1-0

Cover design by: Rachel Dewhurst

Printed in the United States of America

For the City Gate Faithful

God has chosen the foolish things of the world to confound the wise.

1 CORINITHIANS 1:27

CHAPTER ONE

I'm going to begin later in my life, on the banks of the Jordan River in Israel. A great place to start, don't you think? Now try to imagine the scene. There I was, sitting on a bench beside the Jordan and doing my best to understand what had just happened to me in the river. I had been baptized before, but not like that. I was on a tour of Israel, as you no doubt have guessed, and most of the Christians on our two buses wanted to be baptized again, since after all, there we were at the Jordan River. So, why not? I decided to join the rest of the eager bunch.

Well, I was baptized, all right. For the occasion I was wearing one of those white, diaphanous, baptismal gowns. You might have seen them before. They were supplied by the baptizing business on the river bank. Are you ready for this? I doubt it. I wasn't. Our tour leader the night before had suggested we might like to wait a minute before we were dunked. I concluded he was encouraging us to pause, so we might better absorb the essence of the significant spiritual event we were about to enjoy. That might have been his intention, but that's not what happened to me. I didn't have time to do any absorbing of essences. There I was facing the shore and standing waist deep between the two baptizers, when the unexpected definitely happened. Before I could finish saying, "I'd like to wait a min...," I was slam-dunked, and I mean not gently. My feet had suddenly risen from the river bottom without first informing the rest of me of their intention. Up I went and down I came. I made a stunned splash. The two baptizers helped me back to my feet, having been required to do only half a job. I had gone down so fast I didn't have time to close my mouth. I came up sputtering and slobbering the Jordan. A baptizing angel had got the job done.

So there I was sitting overwhelmed on the river bank bleacher, absorbing the peace that passes all understanding and viewing the remaining baptizing proceedings. Baptized by an angel. Might not make a Network TV series. Maybe Netflix. Yes, God does have a sense of humor. The first time I was baptized, thirty-five years before, I came up sputtering, too. And my mouth was open that time, too, even though I'd been given sufficient warning, and I knew, as most people do, you are supposed to close your mouth before you go underwater. And that first time something spiritual happened, too, something freeing. Once I had managed to pull myself up onto the edge of the hotel swimming pool and then to stand, my stomach undulated all by itself and then the peace of God settled on me. I was set free from something. Booze, drugs? The usual suspects, no doubt. So now, sitting on the bank of the Jordan in a cloud of peace, I realized God had reminded me of that first baptism. No deliverance needed this time. Funny, eh?

CHAPTER TWO

God has a sense of humor. I have overwhelming evidence to support that verdict. But don't get me wrong. I'm not saying God is guilty of having a sense of humor. God isn't guilty of anything. God is guilt free. I'm simply saying I have proof He does have one. My life testifies to that. And I'm going to present my evidence to you for verification. Mixed in with my evidence are many of my life's spiritual highlights. In fact, my spiritual highlights are the main focus of this narrative. In addition, I will include insights I've gained over the years about the Kingdom of God. Call it wisdom, if you like. I hope these insights that break into my story won't be too intrusive or unsettling for you. I know a joyful trip is a much preferred way to go. Also, from time to time I will be asking you questions you might like to ponder. For instance, what are your thoughts on the state of the world and the state of the Church? And, of course, you guessed it. I'll be giving you my thoughts on those subjects. You might agree or disagree with my conclusions, but this isn't a test, and you won't find study guides or workbook questions at the end of each chapter. So if you want to give your input on those subjects, then write your own story. This one is mine.

Right now there will be a brief delay in the journey, so I can give you a short summary of some not-so-funny, early-life history, some background to give you a broader understanding of what followed. I'll just get it out of the way. So please wait, this will only take a minute.

I don't really know why it had to happen the way it did for the first 30 years. Life, I mean. It started the way most of us start. In the womb naturally, and then birth and then the years followed. The early ones were mostly a blur. Baseball. I grabbed hold of that early on. I was five, I think. My grandfather stitched a baseball together for me. A brown leather cover with red stitches, fluffy stuffing and a weighted core. I wanted to be a shortstop when I grew up. Didn't we all? Didn't we all want to be something when we grew up? That was the hope we all had, to be something when we grew up. For me life didn't turn out that way for a very long time, about 30 years or so. Thirty lost years when many things were tried, things that led downhill, things that were a long way down from playing shortstop in the Major Leagues. Now I wonder how I survived. There was the alcohol and then there were the drugs. Why did I take that route? Good question. The answer is I didn't see the point. Nobody told me the point of it all. About life, I mean. At least nothing that was believable to me. The point of it all wasn't in the books I read, not in the movies, not on television, not in the alcohol or in the drugs, and not from the people who drank in the bars or from those who took the drugs. No answers were forthcoming, so why would I bother with life at all?

Did I mention the hurts early on? Most people experience hurts along the way. So did I. Maybe more than most. Grandfather, the inspiration for my baseball career, was a pedophile, but why go into that? And mother, a musician, drank. No sense going into that, either. And then there was the high school sweetheart cheerleader, who wanted to go to university alone, meaning without me along to get in the way of her future possibilities. Six months later she was pregnant and married. Ten years after that she was dead. It was cancer. That hurt. There was no sense going to high school reunions after that. But hurts can become less of a burden when numbed by self-medication. And university, who needed that anymore? So you see how life degenerated for me, or more accurately, how I degenerated. But I don't mean to whine; I'm just telling you a few of the highlights of the first thirty years. Suicide? No, I never considered that solution, except to take the slower, more painful way to exit the planet, the coward's way, by living on booze and self-pity.

So where do you want to go from here? You have the option of closing the book on me or you can continue on to hear the rest. As I already mentioned, this isn't a detailed account of my life. This is an account of my spiritual highlights. And if you're wondering about the source of the highlights, the highest light is Jesus. There is no light higher. He turned my life around for me, but not until I was 30 years old and pretty well spent. That's how most of us get there, if we get there at all, those of us who arrive at the truth later in life, when we're all worn out and ready to take the plunge. Most of the Baby Boomers discounted Christianity in their childhood. Church was no longer needed. There was too much going on in the world to bother with Christianity and its choirs and pews and goodie-two-shoes mentality. Who needed it? Most of the Baby Boomers I knew didn't. Whether you were a dropped-out hippy or an establishment lawyer, who needed God when life was so good?

Okay, so what's the real point of writing this? I'll summarize what I already told you. I'm going to relate my spiritual highlights and also highlight God's sense of humor. So is there anyone out there? Is there anyone out there who wants to hear what this life is all about? I mean for real. The topic should be exciting for most humans. Excited or not, I'm going to tell you the answer whether you want to hear it or not. This life is all about our next one. I don't mean some silly reincarnation life, where you might find yourself coming back as an iguana habitually flashing your tongue, or maybe returning as a puffer fish swimming bloated in the ocean. No, we only get one shot at this. And then there's eternity. So how do you want to spend it?

I'm going to lighten up now. As I already mentioned, almost everyone who cares about the subject agrees God has a sense of humor. Call it the joy of the Lord, if you like. Have you noticed humor is a funny thing? What I mean is that many comedians come from miserable backgrounds, and many go to dismal ends. It seems to go with the territory. But there I go again with the sad story. Like I said, failure isn't what I want to tell you about. I want to tell you I made it. And I want to let you know you can make it, too. But again, don't get nervous, this isn't a story of my life. It's a highlighted account of my spiritual history, an account of those times when God has touched me in discernible ways, those experiences when I knew He was real and was guiding me through this life. But don't worry. I'm not going to fill the pages with scripture verses for you to read, so I can expound on them. This journey will be more subtle. Truth will be paraphrased in the narrative and will also be found between the lines. You can do the filling in between the lines if you want to. Also, I'm not going to formally identify my scriptural sources. I will be paraphrasing mostly. Call it plagiarism if you like, but I've never heard of God suing anyone. Zondervan might, but the case would be hard to prove, and I have the best defense attorney there is anywhere, on earth or in heaven. Okay, I'll admit it now. I'm going to identify a few scriptures from time to time. I might even quote a few. You'll hardly notice.

CHAPTER THREE

I began by telling you about my baptism in the Jordan. And before I continue telling you about significant spiritual events in my life, I'd first like to emphasize just how affirming that baptism was. When God sends one of His ministering spirits to ensure a job is done properly, then you can be assured you have been accepted into the beloved. Any doubts you might have entertained in the past are then forever dispelled.

I have had many affirming experiences over the years, including those times when He spoke to me in His still small voice. Those gentle nudges from my Father changed me. When God comes close, He changes a person, but you probably knew that already, unless you're reading this and you don't know Him yet. If that's the case, thank you for reading this far. I'm honored you have taken the time to continue. Most non-believers would have already rejected what I might have to say. We are living in times when most people don't want to hear about it. Did you know in this part of the world we were once the normal ones, and the non-Christians were the maladjusted? Funny, eh?

The first time God came really close to me was in 1977. My wife, Jane, and I were living in a log cabin in Merritt, a small town in the interior of British Columbia. That's right I'm a Canadian. She was teaching school, and I was supposed to be writing something significant, like a great novel. That wasn't happening. So instead, to kill time before bed, I watched the one TV channel still on the air. At midnight the local station ran something called the 700 Club. There was this white guy, Pat Robertson, hosting the show, and his sidekick, Ben Kinchlow, was African American. It was a peculiar show with the white guy and the black guy grinning and oozing joy. Given my frame of reference at the time, I suspected they were both stoned. They were continually happy and wearing goofy grins pasted on their faces. After watching them for a few weeks, I decided to try some of what they were on. I said the prayer. Then I realized I had known him all along, and I had been running away from him for 24 years, ever since I was in that church basement when I was about six. My parents, no doubt hoping to instil some religion into me, tried dropping me off at church on Sundays. That's where I caught a glimpse of Jesus, in a Sunday School Bible story, and I knew He wanted me to follow Him. That prospect was too frightening for me to consider. I left in a hurry and never went back. After my escape I told my parents I didn't want to go anymore, and they didn't press the issue. I guess they thought they didn't have a leg to stand on, since they didn't go themselves. From then on I played in the park on Sundays and snickered at the good kids who were walking by on their way to church.

But at the age of thirty my running had ended, and giving Jesus my life was as easy as falling off a log. But then I was faced with a question. What was I supposed to do next? I had no real Christian experience. I'd come from the pagan pool, as John Wimber, founder of the Vineyard movement, used to call it, so except for my brief brush with God in Sunday School, I was unacquainted with standard Christian behavior. I had to figure out what you were supposed to do when you became a believer, although I did learn some of the basics of the faith from watching the 700 Club. You were supposed to read the Bible and pray. So I started there. And one afternoon soon after my conversion, I was attempting to pray. Naturally enough, I was making the usual requests a person makes. I capped off the end of my prayer with "I love you Lord." In response a still small voice asked me a piercing question. I didn't know where the voice was coming from, whether from inside my head, or from up there near the ceiling somewhere. The voice asked the question, "Yes, but do you love yourself?" I'm still working on that one. Loving yourself can be a two-edged sword. No, the question isn't that simple.

CHAPTER FOUR

Pat and Ben were filled with the joy of the Lord, and that was attractive to me. God drew me to himself through the joy emanating from them, and when I gave my life to the Lord I was filled with joy. Jesus tells us there is rejoicing in heaven when one sinner repents. So heaven must be filled with joy. It has to be. It's heaven.

And then the fun began. You know what I mean, having to go through the whole growth process. The painful character building. The big word for it, of course, is sanctification. We grow by overcoming the world in us and the world out there. There is a lot to overcome here on earth. Heaven is more than wonderful I'm sure, but what about our daily existence down here on this earth? We all need to face the world every day. I wake up in the morning and look around, and here I am again. I'm in the world. I know that fact is not a huge revelation to offer you. I don't expect you to ponder it for too long, since you are in the world, too, and you know all about it. So be assured my insight about being in the world won't be the basis for a book on end time prophecy, complete with timeline. Now getting back to what I was telling you about waking up in the morning. After the sleep fog lifts I begin to think about what my day is going to look like. And maybe my day's prospects aren't too exciting. How about you and your mornings? Try to be honest. How excited are you most mornings about facing the day? As for me, when I consider the essence of my existence, I have to ask myself, why am I not overjoyed every morning over the fact that I'm living in the Kingdom of God? That's right. I'm first of all living in the Kingdom of God. That's where I'm supposed to be living, since I'm one of God's children. Sure, I'm also in the world, but my existence here is only temporary, and so is yours. I try to remember that fact, instead of expecting that my day will simply be more of the same. Did I mention I pastor a church? So when I say, more of the same, I mean no breakthroughs or revival forthcoming today. But then I lighten up and think I might be able to speak a word of encouragement to somebody, or pray for somebody, or do something that actually might make a difference in someone's life. So, how about you? Do you wake up each morning only to discover you are in the world? Of course you do. And then what are you supposed to do about that fact, except face more of the same? And the same old, same old, isn't too exciting most days. But life should be exciting every day, since believers in Jesus are first and foremost living in the Kingdom of God. How about that? When I wake up each morning, I am first of all living in the Kingdom of God. And then I think about those people out there in the world, the ones I am going to see during my day. Most of them are hostile to the name of Jesus, or maybe they might be simply indifferent. How in the world are those people who don't yet know Jesus ever going to come into his Kingdom? When I ask that question, I see Pat and Ben staring me in the face, wearing those goofy grins, and challenging me. If I'm not too excited about being a Kingdom dweller myself, how am I going to bring an authentic message of salvation and the Kingdom of God to those people out there? I need help. But the truth is I'm overwhelmingly blessed with help. Every day I'm carrying God around, wherever I go. What an amazing truth. God, the one who created everything, and also thought I'd make a good companion, created me to carry him around during my remaining time here. What an honor. That's something to be excited about. I need to be excited about that every day. When I wake up each morning, I should be excited about that, no matter what I think might happen next. So I need to ask for the joy of the Lord to come alive in me, since I'm representing the Kingdom of God to the people out there, to the people who are lost. There, I've gone and said it. I've used the word "lost." In some streams of the Church, calling people lost is considered inappropriate. It's not politically correct. It's way too offensive to call people lost. If they are to be called anything, they need to be called pre-salvation people, or something as equally in-offensive. After all, what would they think if they found out I thought of them as lost? I don't want to get a bad reputation. What if they thought I was try-ing to get them found? What if they thought I was try-ing to get them saved? What would the neighbors think of me then? They might think those deluded

Christians next door think we're lost. But when I look around, viewing the world from a Kingdom of God perspective, all I need to do is walk through town, where the people are going about their business, submerged in darkness, and I can plainly see they are lost. Even if they think they know what they are doing and where they are going, if they don't know Jesus, then they are living in darkness, even on a bright sunny day. Before I continue I need to apologize to all those politically correct people who are offended by the word "lost." But if people don't know Jesus, then they are lost. And they need to be saved. Everyone needs to be saved, whether they know it or not.

Most people on earth know what earthly salvation is all about. They know about survival. We can see in popular movies what being saved means to people on earth. In fact, most people will spend a couple of hours watching a movie where people are in peril and waiting for rescue. They need to be saved. And along the way in order to create dramatic tension there are usually events in the story that frustrate the rescue. And most likely a lot of things are blown up along the way, while the story itself doesn't amount to much. Even so, when the two hours end the people are usually rescued and joy ensues. Their lives are saved. A happy ending. Wonder Woman saves the world from everything bad, or the Guardians of the Galaxy save the universe from all that is bad. And there is relief, they are saved, the world will continue. These stories appeal to the need in humanity to be saved. To be saved from danger and evil. They satisfy this need.

I think everyone understands the concept. If people are in peril, then they need to be saved somehow. In the movies the people themselves are usually the ones who manage through their own ingenuity to get themselves saved. The obstacles are overcome by the strength and courage of the people, or a hero arises to save everyone, or maybe the Devil helps them in one way or another, in the guise of the good force, or the good witch, or a supernatural force that isn't God or Jesus. We know, of course, the true Savior isn't allowed in the theater, only the counterfeit ones.

It seems one goal of movies is to indoctrinate the public into accepting the demonic realm. Demons are characterized as well-meaning aliens, who will save us from ourselves, so we won't self-destruct. That's a popular theme these days. But aliens, real or imagined, are simply demons. In our popular culture demons come disguised as aliens. Do you think the concept of aliens might be part of the enemy's plan of deception to bring us all into subjection to him? Millions of unsuspecting people have seen these kinds of movies, the ones promoting the lie that aliens are good and are here to save us. But what's the harm? It's only entertainment. Is it really just entertainment? Yes, the aliens are going to save us. We must accept them as our friends. On the other hand, in many of these stories the aliens turn out to be hostile. And then, of course, humankind rallies, and we save ourselves from evil. Anyone or anything is allowed to save us, except Jesus. He's not allowed to save us. I wonder who promotes that idea. But the salvation of the human race is not to be found in ourselves, or brought to us by aliens. Christians are supposed to be the aliens. We are living in the Kingdom of God. That makes us true aliens in the world. We need to let the truth of the Kingdom of God, in which Christians are living, out. We need to have a revelation of where we are living. We need to come awake. There is inexpressible joy in the Kingdom of God. It's inexpressible because it is supernatural. If heaven is rejoicing over one person's salvation, shouldn't we continually be even more joyful for our own? We've got the best deal in town, and the people out there need to know that. Those people who are lost need to know that. But they won't want to come into the Kingdom if they can plainly see we're not too happy. Of course, we can try to pump up some artificial happiness. But people can see right through us when we pretend. There is a solution though. We have the privilege of appealing to our God for help. We need to ask for the supernatural joy of the Lord to bubble up through us, the supernatural joy that exists in the Kingdom of God. The joy of the Lord comes from the Lord. The joy of the Lord means the joy that comes from Him. And because the joy of the Lord is supernatural, it doesn't depend on our circumstances. In fact, the joy of the Lord can even be present in terrible circumstances. The joy of the Lord is irrational, because it's supernatural. And we don't need to be jumping around in ecstatic rapture to be living in his joy, either. We only need to be in Him. Thank you, Pat and Ben, for introducing me to the joy of my salvation.

CHAPTER FIVE

Salvation is one thing. Church is another. After I was saved, I didn't go to church for about five years. I didn't want to hang out with religious people. Then I fell into a Bible believing, non-denominational, charismatic assembly, and I also began speaking in tongues. Even though it's a contentious issue in the Church, I need to bring it up, because that's what happened to me. Although I do know that our minds can become offended when they are eliminated from conversations between our born-again spirit and God. Okay, so I do know speaking in tongues seems like strange activity. But no matter what our minds might think, tongues are good for us. Scripture tells us so. Anyway, there I was, enjoying my first experience of church, with young people leading worship and people prophesying. Later I discovered not all churches were like that, and I also found out there were religious people carrying on being religious all their lives, and leaving the Holy Spirit out of things altogether. Oh, well.

How's your faith level so far? When the heavenly realm invades this one I know our faith increases, and we become more aware of our true home. The Kingdom of God, which is definitely the spiritual realm, then becomes more of a reality to us. Born-again believers are living in a spiritual Kingdom. God is Spirit, and those who worship Him must worship Him in Spirit and in Truth. We are spirit, soul, and body, and Jesus made it possible by his death on the Cross for us to be born-again into his Kingdom. Our Father in heaven drew us to himself through his son Jesus, and we were convicted of our rebellion against God, and we repented, and we were regenerated in the spirit, born-again into his Kingdom, to live our lives in him. And because Jesus rose again He invites us to share in his life in his supernatural Kingdom.

That sounded preachy to me. But it's the truth. I'll now snap out of my preacher posture and continue telling you about my spiritual highlights, those experiences that changed me, meaning they changed my heart. But translating spiritual experience into our natural language can be a challenge, mostly because it's difficult to use our natural language to communicate the essence and depth of Holy Spirit experience. In other words, I can't somehow make my experience also yours. But by telling you about my experiences perhaps an opening might be created, allowing you also to receive a heart changing touch from the Lord. Although, I do admit that I am apprehensive about relating my experiences, call it the fear of man, if you like. And I do know there is, at worst, the possibility you might just think I'm out of my mind and dismiss my spiritual experience as irrelevant. But since you are still here after reading about my Jordan River baptism, perhaps you're curious to see what's next.

CHAPTER SIX

Okay, so here's a spiritual highlight that underscores God's sublime sense of humor.

In June of 1995, I was planning to go with a group of believers to a conference called The Gathering. It was to be held on Whistler Mountain. If I haven't mentioned it before, I live on Vancouver Island, about a 90-minute ferry ride from the city of Vancouver. Vancouver is on the mainland of British Columbia. Whistler Mountain is about 75 miles north of Vancouver and known for its skiing and snowboarding in the winter and mountain biking and hiking in the summer. You might have heard about Whistler before. It was the sight of the alpine events during the 2010 Winter Olympics.

Anyway, a group of us were supposed to travel over to the mainland in a van one afternoon and arrive prior to the first session that evening. But I was impatient to get there, and decided I wanted to go earlier. I hadn't hitchhiked for about 30 years, and I thought it might be fun to do again. So I rolled my suitcase to the side of the highway and in a few minutes a car pulled over. He drove me 30 miles north and went out of his way to drop me off at the ferry terminal. After I arrived on the mainland, I walked up to the highway leading to Whistler.

There were about a dozen other hitchhikers hoping to thumb a ride. I got in line, thinking this was going to be a long wait. Almost immediately, a 20-ton delivery truck pulled over with a young man driving, and he told me to hop in, having picked me out of the lineup. I told him I was going to a Christian conference at Whistler. He said he was going to Whistler, too. He worked for Whistler Brewing Company. I found myself riding in a beer truck. We had a pleasant conversation on the 90-minute journey, talking about life and faith. I was asked later by the people, with whom I was originally supposed to travel, how I'd managed to get there. I told them the truth. I'd come to the Christian Gathering in a beer truck.

The conference was well attended, and at the end of one of the last sessions the speaker asked us all to stand. He then asked the question, "Who is willing to go?" I told the Lord I was. Immediately, a spiritual air flew toward me. I had my mouth open, as the spiritual air took my breath away. Back at home on Vancouver Island I realized God had commissioned me at that moment on Whistler Mountain, because I had been willing. City Gate Church was founded, and our first public meeting was September 17th, 1995. And incidentally, the young man driving that beer truck, his name was Christian.

So we planted a church in 1995. Now that's funny, planting a church. Did you know planting a church can be fun? Or at least that's what some of those church planting books told me at the time. I must not have planted their prescribed way, since I don't remember church planting as being much fun. People were involved, mostly disgruntled people, who had left other churches because those congregations didn't live up to their expectations. But we were supposed to be different than those others. Many Christians want solid leadership but don't want to be led. They want to influence leadership to go where they want to go. And if you don't meet their expectations, down the road they go again. They would prefer to move on, instead of facing their own issues. Not much fun there. But the church we planted in 1995 is still alive, and, as I enjoy pointing out to the local denominational pastors, we are world headquarters.

For a few years, we belonged to an association of churches, but discovered we had a shallow relationship, so why were we sending them two per cent of our income each year? We left the fold, becoming an independent church. But in order to have some accountability for our members, we decided to form a Pastors' Council. It's an appeal council for the congregation in the event there is immorality or malfeasance committed by the leadership. The council consists of three local pastors. They can be active or retired. So far the council hasn't been called into action. One local, retired pastor of a major denomination asked me what the council duties were prior to signing on. I told him there were no duties, unless he was called upon, and the council hadn't been needed for anything yet. He said, "Then if there's nothing I have to do, count me in."

You might have guessed what variety of believer I

am by now, especially given the title of this book. But, at the same time, I really don't know what a charismatic believer is anymore. Sure, I can give you a definition. What I mean to say is I don't know anymore what label can be pasted to my forehead. I know I'm a Bible believing, Spirit filled Christian. When new people attend on Sunday mornings, they sometimes ask me after the service what kind of church we are. In the past I have tried to give them an answer that defined us. I would say "we're kind of Charismatic-Pentecostal. You know, we were born out of the Charismatic Movement. But now we don't really define our church in that way." That's more or less the stumbling response I would give to that question in the past. It was a self-conscious apology for how we began. But now I'm less likely to apologize for who we are. Instead, I put the onus back onto the person inquiring by simply asking, "We're a Bible believing, Holy Spirit led church. What kind were you looking for?"

City Gate Church, in Duncan, BC, on Vancouver Island, is an outpost of Jerusalem and an outpost of the heavenly Jerusalem. We soldier on. And I'm still the leader. Funny, eh?

CHAPTER SEVEN

City Gate Church hosted conferences in the late nineties. One of them featured Sam Storms, then from Kansas City. He is listed in Wikipedia as: Calvinist, Charismatic, Amillennial, theologian, teacher, pastor and author. David Saunders, a prophetic minister, came along with him. Saunders was slated to help manage Paul Cain's future center, to be called Shiloh Estates in Kansas City, for the training of prophetic ministers. Sam and David had agreed graciously to come all the way from Kansas to our small-town of Duncan, 30 miles north of Victoria, on Vancouver Island. Saunders was recovering from a fractured leg, administered by Storms during a wrestling match. It seems traditional theology and the emerging prophetic ministry were not getting along too well in those days. But when they were here all had been forgiven, though Saunders was still walking with a limp.

As an aside, I want to mention at this point I've got a heart for Americans. I'm sure you've heard a Christian say something like, "I have a heart to pray for this country, or I've got a heart to pray for that institution," or for other areas of life. As a child in the 1950s I played shortstop in Little League and the Brooklyn Dodgers were my team. I was called Little Ricky at the time, since I hadn't started growing yet, so naturally enough the Dodgers' shortstop Pee Wee Reece was my hero. That's when it began. Ever since then I've had a heart for Americans. At first, I thought Canadians and Americans were virtually the same, but I discovered later in life we are not. We have our own distinct national personalities. Anyway, I went on to study American literature and political science at university, and after I was saved I attended many Christian conferences in America. So there you go. I'm a Canadian who has a heart for America and for Americans. Funny, eh?

We hosted the conference at a large, local church, but we decided to hold one evening session on the native reserve. During the meeting the spiritual air was being stirred up, and when Storms got up to speak he was choked off. And it wasn't the Spirit of God doing it. He had to sit down to recuperate. He said later he had never had such an experience in his life. Meanwhile, at the end of the meeting, Saunders wanted to get his picture taken with a native woman he had seen in a dream the night before. He didn't seem to realize, as the picture was being taken, this was the woman who had been doing the witchcraft during the meeting, and the one who had been instrumental in choking off Storms. We then had to reflect later on the wisdom of having a meeting there at the center of the action. Evangelism it was not.

Incidentally, I don't mean to point fingers at the local native people. Witchcraft, in addition to being a work of the flesh, is a demonic spiritual force in our area. The aboriginal people have been victimized by that force. And there are many in the non-native population who engage in occult practices. Thirty miles to the south is Victoria, the capital of British Columbia, where there is a concentration of occult activity and witchcraft among the European descendants, activity which, no doubt, is part of the enemy's strategy to influence government.

City Gate sponsored three Island-wide youth conferences in the late nineties. Youth came from all over Vancouver Island, and the popular youth ministers of the day come to speak. But what we didn't have was the participation of native youth. There was, and still is in our community, a racial divide. One afternoon prior to one of our conferences I saw a native Christian man in the mall, an acquaintance of mine who I knew had teenaged children. I caught up to him, and after we exchanged the usual pleasantries, I asked him if he would encourage his teenagers to attend our conference. This is what he said.

"You know those people, usually farm people, on the prairies who get together when one of them has a need, like they need a new barn or something, something they need help with."

"Sure, I've heard those stories," I said.

"Well, they come together and put up the barn together and they probably eat meals together and when they're done they go back to their own farms until someone else has a need."

"Right," I said.

"Well, you know, those farm people most likely knew each other from before they put up the barn, and they would probably continue knowing each other after they finished putting up the barn."

"Right," I said.

We had a few more words about nothing important, and then we each went our way. His teenagers would not be coming to our youth conference.

CHAPTER EIGHT

We have all heard about the love of God. I experienced His love first hand in 1986. I was in the hospital for a medical procedure that required prior fasting. As I lay on the gurney in the hall, waiting to be taken into the operating room, I was concerned and anxious about the outcome, so I was praying earnestly in the Spirit. And as the nurse came to wheel me in I was engulfed in what I would describe as golden, liquid, love honey. The glory of God was so strong I was unable to separate my fingers. In God's presence my fear was saturated in his love and cast out. His presence was so strong and wonderful I wanted to reach out and let the nurse share in my ecstatic state.

I extended my hand to her and gushed, "Here, feel this." But she only looked at me as if the anesthetic was causing my peculiar, if not potentially rude behavior, but then she looked at me again, realizing I hadn't had any medication yet.

And that large polyp the doctor snipped off, it turned out to be benign.

Much later, in 2015, I had a dream about the love of God. I'm not able to describe to you the experience in a way that would communicate to you its full effect on me. The best I can do is try. His love was the safest, securest place to be. I was immersed in the unconditional love of God, a place where a person would just love to stay. People who have died and gone to heaven, I mean those who actually have been there, and then have come back again, often report the same kind of experience, except their experience is usually more intense to the degree that they didn't want to come back.

In 2016 I was attending a conference and at one point in an evening session the speaker asked ministry leaders to stand and then asked others to gather around and pray for us. As people prayed for me, I felt my legs had become spiritual tree trunks, solid, sturdy, unwavering. I was rooted there. Members of the Body of Christ were praying for me, and as they prayed I became rooted and grounded in love. The experience communicated to me that my position in Christ, in the Body of Christ, with Jesus as the head, is to be rooted and grounded in his love. He is the power upholding us all. My legs in my human strength would never be strong and solid enough to endure to the end. But in the power of his love I'm able to stand.

The experience of God's love is difficult to share with people. If you have experienced God's love, have you ever tried to describe the essence of that love to others? We can try, but our communication is fallen, and so are we. That means our language is inadequate when we try to communicate spiritual truths. We live in this fallen state, and we use, and God uses in his book, a fallen medium of communication to communicate His truth to us. He is communicating with us on our fallen level of existence, using words we know in our natural language. And when we are born-again of the Spirit, our line of communication is opened to the Father. We then have the opportunity to communicate on a spiritual level. God is communicating with us in our English language through his word and also by his Spirit. The word of God and the Spirit of God come together. When God's word is enlivened by his Holy Spirit and we compare spiritual things with spiritual, we gain a deeper understanding of what we are doing here, a deeper understanding of what our purpose is in this life. Before we came alive in the Spirit, scripture was only words. We might have had an intellectual understanding of the words. In fact some who aren't born-again have written books on scripture from an intellectual viewpoint and have made some sense of it. I had an English professor at University whose main area of study was the New Testament. In fact, he wrote books on the New Testament. He was a highly respected scholar. As a student he was allowed to skip over his Master's Degree. He went straight from his Bachelor's Degree to his Doctorate. I talked to him one afternoon over coffee in the student cafeteria. He knew about the born-again experience. He knew it all. The only thing he said he couldn't do was take a leap of faith. I guess his mind wouldn't let him. He seemed content to live in his head.

The truth is unless we have the Holy Spirit bringing life to the words, then words are all they are. That's not to say the Bible isn't true just as it stands. But as wonderful as scripture is, how great its depth, how true its meaning, it is, nevertheless, a primer, a beginners course given to us to point us to Jesus and the hope of eternal life with, and in, Him. Of course, eternal life is incomprehensible from where we are now. And God's love for us is hard for us to grasp. What does that word "love" mean anyway? On earth we have various meanings attached to it, which brings confusion, since those meanings are tied to this earth. We know love is something we are told to aspire to. People generally agree with that. But Jesus used the word to convey a much higher meaning. And since there is no word in the many languages of this world to describe God adequately, we say God is love. But again, what does that mean? It must be the eternal presence of God that is being described. The love of God transcends the word we use. In other words, God's heart for us is far beyond anything we can conceive of here on earth. In fact, I suspect "love" isn't even what we think it is, because we have attached human connotations to it. God's presence and our life in his Kingdom are what we really want. We say God is love, but it is really his presence we want to live in. It's him we want to be with, to be in relationship with. The essence of God and the atmosphere of his Kingdom are what we want. And in our limited capacity to understand, we use the word "love." But God is way bigger than our word "love."

Love is used many times in scripture to describe to us this characteristic of God. But it is used in order for us to try to understand that the way things are in the Kingdom of God are not the way things are here in this world. The thing called love can only be lived in the Kingdom of God. To live in the essence of what is called love we need to have the source of that love in our lives. And that source is Jesus. Without Jesus there is no love for us. People in the world can express human love, which is limited in its capacity, but real love, or what the word "love" represents, can only be found in Jesus. And in our eternal future we will know him and one another. We will be living in the essence of what our word "love" inadequately describes. The word love is a shallow attempt to describe the real thing. This sense of love we experience here gives us a hint of home, a home of love, peace, and joy. Love has its earthly meaning, but when referring to God, it's just a word we use here on earth to describe the unknowable. The state of "being in love" will only be known when we live there, and then the word love we use here will no longer be needed, because He simply is.

CHAPTER NINE

I could burden you with the many supernatural events the enemy has initiated over the years to attack me and our community of believers. The opposition has been at times intense but by the grace of God unsuccessful. I don't want to focus too much on the Devil's schemes. But to give more depth to my story, I will tell you about a few of those encounters in the hope you might find my insights helpful.

As you know there is a lot of evil in the world, mostly inspired by an untold number of evil beings in the spiritual realm. That evil, of course, preys on our fallen nature. And even though the Devil is only allowed to do what we agree to, we do manage to agree to a lot. Anyway, here's a true life example of a demonic attack.

In the early nineties I was walking through our local mall, when I was hit by an invisible weight that bowed my head, and I felt sick to my stomach. The words, "this is a spiritual attack," went through my mind. I asked my son to get my wife, who was in the grocery store, while I waited on one of the mall benches. She came and took me to the hospital. In the emergency room the nurses took one look at me and plunked me in a wheelchair. It seems my face was a shade of green. They laid me out on a gurney, took some blood, and stuck those wired white discs on me in several locations. There I lay, a beached whale. My son didn't look too happy about the situation. All the tests came back negative. I was just fine. Although afterward I was in bed for several days, apparently sick with no cause. A local pastor who had years of experience with native witchcraft told me one of the aboriginal practitioners had shot a curse at me, likely coming from the McDonald's restaurant I was passing at the time. You can believe his spiritual explanation or not. Either way, such events are hard to prove one way or the other. But as disagreeable as the experience was, I'm happy to say the enemy hasn't discouraged me from patronizing McDonald's.

So right now you might be thinking I'm reading too much into events, and maybe I should limit my speculations to earthly reality and simply take events at face value. Don't go too deep. Don't get too complicated. Don't be so spiritual. Don't go looking for demons behind every bush. Stay in this earthly reality. Take life at face value. You'll be happier that way.

You might have noticed that our lives these days are controlled mostly by screens. A majority of us are now captivated by our electronic devices. We devote much of our time engaged with the surface of things.

Looking at the surface of things is not exclusive to our day. People in the days of Paul the apostle also looked at surfaces. We know that fact because Paul wrote to the people in Corinth, telling them they were judging him only by his appearance. They were unable to see below the surface and see the spiritual truth of who he was. We might ask the question today, how is the Church generally doing when it comes to appearances? Are we dazzled by the idols of personality? Do we need to come awake, so we can see the condition we are in, individually and collectively, just below the surface? Does the Church need to be revived, to come alive to the truth, to come alive to what is going on in the Church and in the world right now? To come awake so we can see, so we can see below the surface of things.

We need to come awake to see God's Kingdom and be aware of his government and not be deceived by counterfeits. There is much pretension in the world and in the Church, and these deceptions have been established to substitute for the true knowledge of God. But that's where we need to live, in the true knowledge of God. Some segments of the Church present a form of Godliness for all to see but won't allow the Holy Spirit to come in and lead. Meanwhile, many who are lost in the world might see the Church as just another institution, occupying a building and having stained glass windows. And everyone knows now that stained glass makes a colorful addition to wedding videos. But that's not what God intended his Church to be. The body of Christ needs to be able to discern counterfeit Godliness, and reject its expression. We need to live deeper lives and reject the surface of things. There is no power in a form of Godliness. Our God is powerful and will not be contained in a form suitable for those people who are living a spiritually superficial life in a superficial Church, where the power of the Holy Spirit of God is not allowed to attend. When the power of God is not allowed into an assembly of believers, then we might wonder if God is there at all. When people are in charge of a form they call church, where Father, Son, and Holy Spirit are not well known or welcome, then the result is a superficial expression of religion.

But the question might arise, why go deeper anyway? After all, there is enough to contend with in this world. Making a living takes up most of our time, and we also need to endure all the things the world throws at us. We don't have time to go deeper. If that is our attitude then we don't know or understand our true need. We are then lost in a form of church, living our Christian lives on the surface. We are assured of salvation, of course, but we are effectively useless in ministering the love and power of God to the people out there. Those people out there most likely do think of the Church as an institution and a building. No help to be found there. But in fact people are in great need of spiritual reality, and they need to be saved from the things of this world that have taken them captive. They need Jesus. He is love, and He is powerful. The Church needs to know him deeply.

The Corinthians saw only the surface of Paul. They saw him as timid and unimpressive in person, and thought his speaking amounted to nothing. They only saw the surface of Paul. And even though the gifts of the Spirit were active in their church, in their immaturity they were unable to comprehend Paul's authority in Christ. How is the Church doing today?

Today we see that people in our world are kept busy looking at surfaces. We are captured by the surfaces of film and video, and computer screens. We have I-Pads and other tablets, on which we can experience the surface of people. Sadly, we often call these surface communications our relationships. And we have, of course our ubiquitous cell phones. People bury themselves in their surfaces, captivated by images on a screen. And at the same time we are being screened by others, mostly for the purpose of selling us something.

Microsoft has a device, advertised as a tablet with the power of a laptop. It's called Surface, and the company now has a whole line of models to choose from. Just imagine, if we all had one, we could go surfing on the Surface. Let's all surf on the Surface and be somebody. And it's not just the young people who are transfixed by technology. I saw a couple, most likely in their eighties, who were sitting at a table at noon in a local restaurant. They were dressed like they had come from a Sunday morning church service. They sat down, and each immediately took out their cell phone and began to ignore each other.

There is no real community to be had on the surface. There can be no deep relationships formed, as people skip on the surface from relationship to relationship, often using dating services or worse, as they live on the surface of things, which will ultimately lead to a superficial life and captivity to a system of surfaces. Of course, we do know these devices also can be useful if they are not dictating our lives and demanding our attention, but when taken to the extreme can become idols.

If you think I am exaggerating, did you know there is a new religion, a new religion of artificial intelligence called *Way of the Future*? Coming straight from Silicon Valley, its focus is on "the realization, acceptance, and worship of a godhead based on artificial intelligence (AI) developed through computer hardware and software." The leader of the new religion and the CEO of the nonprofit corporation formed to run it had papers filed with the Internal Revenue Service in May of 2017. The leader is Anthony Levandowski who says "...what is going to be created will effectively be a god. It's not a god in the sense that it makes lightning or causes hurricanes. But if there is something a billion times smarter than the smartest human, what else are you going to call it?" Here we see the potential for total captivity. We can worship a god we humans have created.

Have you ever wondered why people don't get it? Why don't people understand how this whole Church thing is supposed to be? Why don't people understand this is a spiritual event?

God is Spirit and those who worship him must worship him in Spirit and in truth. Why don't people understand the Church needs to come into proper order for the Kingdom of God to advance?

Or maybe you're one of those who doesn't get it yet. If that's the case, you might ask, what's "it," anyway? "It" is having your heart captivated by God, with Jesus dwelling in the center of your heart, a heart that is aching for more of him. That ache wants to search the heart of God and go far below the surface of things. The Corinthian church was shallow. So shallow they didn't know or recognize true spiritual authority. They were judging by appearances, on the surface. Immature people were commending themselves and measuring one another by superficial, immature standards. In our day, we might ask, is the religious establishment classifying and comparing themselves with one another? Are they doing their best to perform in order to climb the ecclesiastical ladder? Are they focused on who has the biggest church? Or the most people, or who has the finest, most technologically advanced sound system? Is that the way true spiritual authority is supposed to behave?

Looking on the surface of things has been ingrained in the people of this world and become their common way of life. And the Church is not exempt from this kind of worldview. We often bow down to celebrity, rather than follow those in genuine spiritual authority. And we know where that has led us. In the Church we can even talk spiritual talk and teach spiritual principles, but often we are only touching the surface of God's truth. We look at scripture from various angles so we can say we have learned something, instead of facing a basic issue such as living a crucified life. We talk about the Cross and then even agree with the necessity of going there, but how many actually take the trip? We need to be revived to know the deep things of God. Do we think the word of God would tell us there is such a thing as the deep things of God, if we weren't supposed to begin to know the deep things of God? Do we want to be revived, so our eyes, our ears, and our hearts are opened to know who we are and who God created us to be? Do we want to break the mold we are in right now? Do we want to break out of the cultural conditioning we have been subjected to? To go beneath the surface? If we are willing, then the Holy Spirit will break us out and will make us alive to know the deep things of God, and to know Him and the power of his resurrection.

CHAPTER TEN

In 1998, a few of us from City Gate went to a MorningStar conference in Charlotte, North Carolina, hosted by Rick Joyner. We arrived early to one of the afternoon meetings and managed to get seats in the front row. The worship that afternoon was out of this world. I actually got up and danced. Then we sat down to hear the scheduled speaker. I was sitting there immersed in the glory of God, when I heard the voice of Bob Jones say from a row to my left, "smell the fragrance of the Lord." And I did. It smelled to me like incense and vanilla, and it was intoxicating in the best sense of the word. There was no mistaking it. So there I was in the front row immersed in God's glory and breathing in that heavenly aroma. Then Steve Thompson, one of the MorningStar pastors rose to the platform to introduce the afternoon's speaker. After failing on several attempts to form words, he realized he was unable to talk and slumped onto the podium. Two ushers, seeing his predicament, cautiously went up to the platform and helped him down to his seat. Then the afternoon's speaker, Don Potter, ascended the platform and attempted to begin his teaching on worship. He also discovered he was unable to talk. Then he realized he was able to sing. So he sang his whole teaching. I sat there bundled up in the love of God, the aroma of vanilla and incense filling the air around me. I would have been content to remain in that peace and presence of God for the remainder of my life, but Potter's teaching and the meeting ended. Later, as I sat in the lobby reviewing what had happened in the meeting, the incense and vanilla fragrance still lingered in the air around me. At a later meeting, the same aroma enveloped me. Bob Jones said angels were gathering, and they would be going home with those attending the conference. I then began to associate the fragrance of incense and vanilla with angels. After the conference ended, we flew from Charlotte to Toronto, and then on to Vancouver. Waiting at the gate to fly from Vancouver to Victoria, the fragrance of the Lord again surrounded me. To ensure the aroma wasn't coming from some other source, such as Starbucks, I scanned the area. But no, the incense and vanilla fragrance had returned. And since I hadn't smelled the fragrance in Toronto, I theorized the angels hadn't bothered taking the trip to Toronto but had flown straight to Vancouver. A few years later, I told the story one evening to our weekly men's group at a local coffee shop. As I spoke the atmosphere in the room began to brighten in the Spirit, as the angels, sent to those who will inherit salvation, were making themselves known and confirming my account. The angels are here with us and under orders to advance God's Kingdom.

CHAPTER ELEVEN

The Bible tells us the truth about how we are to live and what this life is really all about. But in the unsaved world, humans have ways of constructing various realities to live by. You've heard about myths. We most often think of them as historical legends, which are usually jam-packed with action and adventure. But there is another definition of the word. A myth can also be defined as an invented idea, or concept. To be more precise a myth is a belief or set of beliefs, often unproven or false that have accrued around a person, phenomenon, or institution.

If people don't know the truth, that is, if they don't know Jesus, they can only fabricate an existence by establishing a myth to live by. Myths can be established by adopting various philosophies, or isms, or religions, or relationships to believe in. If people are not living in the truth, then they need to invent something to live for, or by. Or they need to copy someone else's myth, someone who has an ideology or concept of the world that isn't the truth. If Jesus is excluded from their lives, then they don't have the truth, since Jesus is the Truth. As I already mentioned, I was a lousy myth maker for my first 30 years. I didn't know how to create or sustain one. And all the myths being marketed in my formative years didn't make sense to me, and some were ridiculous. My myth making failure meant I was a failure. The world told me so, and I was in complete agreement. There was nothing else for me to do but drop out of society entirely. The myths were of no use. And I didn't find the truth at the bottom of the bottle, or in the acrid smoke, either. But I knew I needed to find the answer fast, before I sank into the abyss. And then God rescued me with the truth. He saved me. I had looked everywhere. But when He saved me I didn't need to look any further. When I found the Truth, there was nowhere else I needed to go. Jesus is the answer. The Truth is the Truth. No more myth making required. I don't need to fabricate or hold onto myths about myself, because I am living the truth of what being alive here on earth is all about. He created me to love him with all I am, and to tell others the truth of what being here is all about. Any attempt to live solely for myself is bound to fail, because I won't be living the truth.

Jesus is the absolute truth, but you might have noticed absolutes aren't wanted these days. And the definition of tolerance seems to have changed, too. It has been altered slightly. Now Christians not only have to be tolerant of the religious beliefs of others, but now we have to agree their ways are as good as ours. Christians by definition can't agree to that. Can we see where this is headed, unless God intervenes?

CHAPTER TWELVE

I mentioned earlier about waking up in the morning to face the world out there. The world wants me to believe the lie. There are many voices in the world, and there are various ways the Devil communicates the lie to us. I try to differentiate among those voices and communications in order to discern who is speaking. Discernment is required. Hearing and discernment are crucial, because the world out there is filled with lies. The world system promotes the lies, and the people who live in that system, and who are committed to that system, believe the lies. There are many variations of the lie. You can find most of them on the Internet. The world wants people to believe the lie. But how can I tell people the truth, if I, myself, am infected with the lie?

There was a movie released in 1998 titled *The Truman show*, starring Jim Carrey. It was all about the lie. It was about living in the lie, and it's a big lie. In the movie the lead character, 30-year-old Truman Burbank, is unaware his entire life is a hugely popular 24-hour-a-day TV series. Truman, the product of an unwanted pregnancy, was adopted at birth by the TV network and raised in the zoo-like environment of a TV soundstage. And every moment of Truman's existence is captured by concealed cameras and telecast to a huge global audience. He lives in the cheerful community of Seahaven, an island "paradise" where the weather is always mild and no unpleasantness intrudes. And his wife, his friends, and his family are all actors. Over the years, the Truman show becomes a billion-dollar franchise for the TV network. Truman, of course, doesn't know he's a prisoner on an immense, domed, city-size soundstage that simulates his home of Seahaven. But if Truman were ever to discover the truth and leave Seahaven then both the illusion and the ratings would collapse. In addition to the elaborate events staged to ensure he doesn't try to leave Seahaven, Truman is given constant reminders of how wonderful his island paradise is compared to the dangers lurking in other parts of the world. But his growing suspicions eventually make him curious enough to want to leave, and the show's director and master manipulator, Christof, must constantly devise ways to frustrate Truman's escape attempts. And the movie carries on from there toward the conclusion, toward a happy ending or a sad one.

I think you can see the point I'm making here. Truman was told a huge lie, and he lived in that lie from birth onward. And that lie was called reality. For him it was reality. Truman believed the reality he was living in was true. But it was a lie, which prompts the question, "Does Truman's story have any application to people's lives in our world today?" We might at least consider the possibility that the majority of the people in the world are living in a Seahaven reality. They have believed a lie about what reality is and what the truth is. And most of the world's population live under a dome of lies, just as Truman did. And God, the Creator of all, is hidden by the dome of lies promoted by the world system, which is under the direction not of Christ of, but of the Devil. The truth, the truth about reality is concealed by the Devil's dome of lies and consists of spiritual strongholds, vain philosophies, false religions, and is designed to keep people lost and ignorant in their sin and rebellion. The world has a strong hold on the people in it, and the dome of deception is designed and constructed to keep the world living under a lie.

The Devil promotes the lie. There is a Devil. He doesn't frolic around in a red suit, swinging a tail behind him and sporting horns on his head. Hollywood promotes that kind of image. But, in fact, he is a fallen cherub and can be mistaken for an angel of light. Tricky, eh?

But just so we don't get too comfortable judging the lost, who have believed the Devil's lies, there are people in churches who believe religious lies. Here's one: Live a good life and you'll go to heaven when your soul-directed life has ended. You don't need to be born-again, and you can leave the Holy Spirit outside the church door. It's all good. Jesus paid the price for your trip to heaven. Grace, grace. Live like hell if you like. You're covered. But that is a religious lie.

In the end those living in the lie will awaken to discover their existence has been hollow and fruitless. To be satisfied and content living in the myth of Seahaven is folly.

CHAPTER THIRTEEN

Here's another example of a spiritual attack, re-sulting from a white lie. There's no such thing as a white lie, but I'll call it that. There are no white witches, either. A lie is a lie, and a witch is a witch. So here's what happened. Our Labrador retriever went missing one morning. We later received a call from a couple on the native reserve. They said she had fol-lowed them home. I asked for their address and went to fetch Meg. When I got there I realized they ex-pected to receive a reward. I told them Meg was my wife's dog, and I that I was sure she would want to give them something for finding her. I knew I was telling a big lie, because I knew, and my wife knew, they likely had not discouraged Meg from going with them. After I left their home, I began to experience the world around me shaking, and my vision flutter-ing. This continued for a day or more. Finally, I de-cided to go to the grocery store and buy a turkey as a reward for finding Meg. I took them the turkey, for which they were thankful, and the shaking and flut-tering stopped. Lying is a bad idea. White man spoke with forked tongue, and the demonic realm took full advantage of the opening.

You might be starting to think my bizarre spiritual accounts are springing from a troubled mind. Or if you are inclined to be generous and kind, perhaps you might interpret them as unfortunate tales, resulting from pastoral burnout. Or if you are more judgmental, you might decide I'm simply loony. Whatever your opinion might be of these events, you might want to acknowledge there is a demonic spiritual realm all around us. I've read about that certainty in the Bible.

The demonic realm is real. Here is evidence to support that fact. Our city celebrates a festival every year in July, called Duncan Days. There is a parade and there are various events that draw people into town. City Gate's sanctuary is in a former theater, and we share the building with several businesses, including a New Age, occult gift store. And every year the psychics have their tables set up in the hall leading to City Gate's entrance. There for a fee they give their tarot and other kinds of readings. One year, a few weeks after Duncan Days had ended I received a call from a retired pastor/missionary, whom I'd never met. He told me he and his wife ran a curio shop in town. Across the hall from his business was a café, and he phoned to tell me he had overheard a conversation two people were having over tea in the café. The two fortune-tellers were talking about their occult readings during the festival and saying the power had been weak, and they had difficulty hearing because of the pastor and the church at the end of the hall. He had phoned to congratulate me on a job well done and encouraged us to keep up the good work.

His phone call reminded me that we are in a continual territorial battle. The power of the enemy is always at work. And his power leads to darkness and death. But the power of God gives us power to live our lives, and guarantees our future and our safety. City Gate has been in the same location since the year 2000. God has given us the power to survive, and to be a light in the face of darkness and hostile forces, as we overcome the work of the enemy in the truth and power of Christ's victory.

CHAPTER FOURTEEN

Now, if you are really beginning to think my Christian life is a little off-center, here is an event to support your opinion. I might as well get it out of the way right now. And for those who like to swim in the sober, religious stream of Christianity, you might want to skip these next two paragraphs lest your teeth begin to grind involuntarily. I'm only thinking of your welfare.

I had my head in Winnipeg once. Just my head. Winnipeg is the longitudinal center of Canada. It happened this way. A married couple on City Gate's Leadership Team went for a holiday in the Maritimes on Canada's east coast. When they were there they decided to bring back a jar full of the Atlantic Ocean. In the late '90s we had a group of pastors on Vancouver Island attending monthly Island Fire Renewal meetings, so I decided to take the bottle of Atlantic water to one of those meetings. During our lunch break, one of the pastors suggested we go to the harbor and get some water from the Pacific. The plot thickened from there. After lunch we decided to place the water in two bowls in front of the church platform. Our idea was to pray for Canada, with the water symbolizing our nation from sea to sea. So far, so good. And since I had brought the Atlantic water to the meeting and thus had been the inspiration for this event, I was commissioned to go first. I approached the platform, knelt, and placed my right hand in the Atlantic bowl of water and my left in the Pacific. That's when the unexpected happened. Suddenly, and I mean suddenly, I found myself standing on my head, my right hand in the Atlantic and my left in the Pacific, my head in Winnipeg.

I wasn't accustomed to standing on my head. It was not my preferred position. I stayed up there, precariously, until my prophetic purpose for being upended had ended. Once down I was unable to get up from the floor, and I stayed there for an extended period of time, with one prophetic brother beside me prophesying about something to do with Canada, but what specifically I don't remember, as the others took their turns at the bowls. Incidentally, I've never actually been to Winnipeg. I've heard it's very cold there. Funny, eh?

Before I was saved, I didn't understand religious people. I still don't. When I was a sinner I went at sin full bore. When I finally discovered the Truth, I went just as hard in His direction. Being good and religious has never had any attraction for me. I'm in a relationship with Jesus. He's not religious either. So what is the deal with religion?

We in the Church can get too cozy pointing our fingers at the world and its demonic influences. Instead we might want to recognize the reality of the demonic spiritual realm also operating in the Church. The most prevalent influence is the religious spirit. It controls and manipulates, preventing believers from being effective in the world. The religious Church is mostly centered on erecting a righteous façade for its members, who then receive praise from one another instead of from God. Jesus tells us in John 5:42, "But I know you, that you do not have the love of God in you. I have come in My Father's name, and you do not receive Me; if another comes in his own name, him you will receive. How can you believe, who receive honor from one another, and do not seek the honor that *comes* from the only God?"

If the religious spirit can keep Christians living in their own name and thinking they are being the Church, then its mission is accomplished. If I accept those who come in their own name, especially when they are leaders in the religious establishment, then it's okay if I also stay in my own name. And then I don't have to lose my life to gain it. Meanwhile, the religious establishment is in trouble, and for many in leadership the key to survival is to compromise and become more like the world. But Jesus asks us if we can even believe, if we accept glory from one another instead of receiving our approval from God.

Seeking and accepting praise from one another, instead of from God, perpetuates a religious system and attitude. What we really need to do is lose our lives, to be in Jesus, and to come in his name. We can't be His body if we aren't living our lives in him. We can't believe if we seek glory from men. Receiving glory from men allows us to belong to an established religious system, indwelt by the spirit of religion, where we don't need to lose our lives. We only need to lose enough of our lives to maintain our salvation. The Church in North America has generally become a congregation of well-educated spectators. Jesus says unless we lose our lives to gain his, we will be an easy victim of the religious spirit, which will conspire to keep us in its grip.

For a few years now I have considered starting a new course similar to Alpha. It's called Omega. Participants are required first to come into the Kingdom of God and die, and then carry on from there. I don't know how many people would be interested in taking the course, since the accepted religious system says it's okay to love your life here on earth more than you love the Lord.

The insidious schemes of the religious spirit need to be exposed. This isn't a minor issue, such as what color the hymnal should be, or whether we should have pews or chairs, or a worship team, or a pipe organ, or a choir, or meet in a cathedral, or in a converted movie theater. No, exposing the religious spirit is more crucial than that. The religious spirit leaves the Church powerless. The Church needs to break out of the bondage the religious spirit has wrapped her up in.

We have been indoctrinated into a dysfunctional system that tells us the Church is supposed to be a certain way. One fallacy promoted by the spirit of religion is that the Christian's role is to come to church to be served. The notion that the congregation needs to be served is usually promoted by church leadership. Of course, there are those who need to be served, those who are in need. But that's not what I mean. I'm talking about the general state of our church culture.

The prevailing aim of church leadership is to serve the people, so they won't go to another church to have their needs met. That means the goal for leadership is to serve the congregation so well with programs and self-help methods that they stay in the fold, being served, and having no real spiritual goal in mind except to go to church and live a happy Christian life, instead of being equipped for service. And at the same time be glutted with teaching without application. Most don't even know they need to be equipped for service. The Church needs to come together in ways that do equip us for service, not in ways that serve the religious establishment. Of course, when people leave one church and go elsewhere the leadership of the church they left is offended by the leaders of the church they go to, and consequently walls of separation in the body of Christ are reinforced.

There are also those who live their lives outside of a church community, those who haven't been able to live in the religious system. They know there is something wrong, but they don't quite know what it is. They are usually the ones hungering for more of God, who have escaped the system, and then find themselves wandering around, searching for the right place to be, and wondering, what is wrong? Or they have given up wondering and have given up on Church altogether.

If the religious spirit is in control, it doesn't matter what form the church structure takes, either, from house-churches to liturgical, the result will be the same. If believers in Christ don't love the Lord more than they love their lives here on earth, they are prime targets for the religious spirit and the domination of those who are coming in their own name. And, of course, if Christians are coming in their own name, they will find someone or some group to lead them who are also coming in their own name. I follow Paul, I follow Apollos. I follow the pastor, who will take care of my spiritual life for me. But of course that's not possible. We can't have someone else make the sacrifice for us. No one else can do it for us. How can I pray in the name of Jesus unless I do give up my life for Him?

Think about it. How did we end up this way? This isn't the scriptural model of Church. The saints need to be equipped for the work of the ministry. And equippers are required. If we are complaining about the Lord not answering our prayers, we might wonder why not? Jesus tells us in John 16:23, "And in that day you will ask Me nothing. Most assuredly, I say to you, whatever you ask the Father in My name He will give you. Until now you have asked nothing in My name. Ask, and you will receive, that your joy may be full."

If we don't know him well enough, if we don't know his word, if we don't know his heart, then we aren't in him. And if we are not praying the Lord's will, we are coming in our own name. In our own name we will most often pray primarily for our own hopes and desires. When we say we have given our lives to the Lord, we need to mean it and let him be the one to change us. Our prayers in his name aren't prayers in his name, if He isn't in agreement with them, and if we don't really know him.

The disciples asked Jesus to teach them to pray. Thy Kingdom come, thy will be done, on earth as it is in heaven. Not our Kingdom come, and our will be done, on earth as it is on earth. The spirit of religion would keep us praying in our own name.

When we pray in our own name, we are saying we love our lives here more than we love the Lord. And the spirit of religion would keep us that way. And if we don't want to give our lives completely to God, we will hire someone who, presumably, will represent us in spiritual matters. Then we will have ritualized submission, which will be, in truth, only superficial. Then we can resume going about the business of running our lives our own way, and keeping God at a distance, since He is so hard to know anyway.

And as I already noted, if the Devil can set up an institution that looks like, and is called the Church, one we can run ourselves, instead of allowing the Holy Spirit to be in charge, then for the Devil it is mission accomplished. Then the great commission will not be fulfilled. We can't introduce the nations to a God we don't know ourselves. We can only tell the lost what we know about him and convert them to religion. Here's the bottom line: Do we love our lives more than we love him? He didn't love his life here more than He loves us. Put another way, can we say,

"I love him more than I love me?" Love is sacrificial. We sacrifice our love of our own lives for him, and then we sacrifice for others. If the Church actually was that way, the Church would be dangerous. Then we would be living the greatest commandment, as Jesus instructs us in Mark 12:28, "...you shall love the Lord your God with all your heart, with all your soul, with all your mind, and with all your strength.' This is the first commandment. And the second, like it, is this: 'You shall love your neighbor as yourself.' There is no other commandment greater than these." And then we would be equipped to fulfill the great commission Jesus has given to us: "Go therefore and make disciples of all the nations, baptizing them in the name of the Father and of the Son and of the Holy Spirit." Matthew 28:19-20

We know from history when Christians are martyred, the Church expands under such persecution. Why? Christian martyrdom is the ultimate statement. Those saints who were martyred didn't love their lives here more than they loved the Lord. They lived their lives in his name.

"Most assuredly, I say to you, unless a grain of wheat falls into the ground and dies, it remains alone; but if it dies, it produces much grain." John 12:24

They died in his name and by their sacrifice they produced much grain and the Kingdom of God was advanced.

We need to change our minds, and go from spectator to participant, and expel the religious spirit from our lives.

CHAPTER FIFTEEN

The question is often asked, why isn't everyone healed? Let's just say it's a big subject we won't go into right now. In the meantime, I'll tell you about my experience with sickness. I was bitten by a tick in 1982 that left me feeling martyred while still alive. I now categorize the event as an enemy attack. The engorged arachnid had been feeding on the back of my right thigh. That's where I found it. The rash showed up later. Nobody was talking about Lyme Disease in 1982. Then the fun began. Fever, chills, you know, the regular ills, and then the muscle and joint pain, and severe fatigue. I remember my father-in-law cutting our grass because I couldn't get out of bed. No son-in-law wants that. My doctor tested me for mononucleosis, and then he decided I had Multiple Sclerosis. One afternoon he asked my wife to come and join us in his examination room to give us his assessment. We weren't pleased with his diagnosis. Multiple Sclerosis he said. He then sent me to the University Hospital for a spinal tap to confirm his diagnosis. No, doc, you were wrong, but the needle in my back was memorable. Then in 1990 I saw Ted Koppel on ABC's Nightline airing a segment on Lyme disease. And there was the rash, in living color. Too late for antibiotics, unless I wanted to kill every bacterium in my body, both bad and good. Over time I attended more than a few Christian conferences trying to receive a healing touch. That didn't happen. And it hasn't yet, but at the same time I've learned along the way a lot about the ministry of healing.

In 1990, I went to Kansas City for a conference hoping to be healed. One of the seminars was on fasting, taught by Mahesh Chavda, who had extensive fasting experience. When he ended his teaching, he said he would pray for those who needed healing. I stood in the long line and watched him coming closer, as people were hitting the deck gently in his wake, lowered by trained catchers. The deck was a cement floor. He came to me and asked me what I wanted prayer for. I told him the problem, and he commanded the plague to come out of me. I'd never fallen over before, but this time I fell. But no one caught me. I guess the word "plague" had discouraged the catchers. In their defense, they might have thought the plague was AIDS. The floor was hard, but I forgave them. Then it happened. My right arm began to bounce on the cement floor all by itself, as electric shocks were twitching my elbow. I'll explain to you why that was happening by giving you some of my elbow background. A few years earlier my son in grade one was diagnosed with Legg Perthes Disease. For six months he had to be in casts on both legs to hold his hips in place. A bar connected the casts at the knees, leaving his legs spread wide. I picked him up by the bar to carry him, and I developed chronic pain in my elbow. So there I was on the cement floor, my arm bouncing. When the electric shocks stopped, so did the pain. I sensed God saying, "You carried your son around. I'm carrying you." But the Lyme "plague" remained. He wasn't healing plagues that day.

Healing. It's a tough and touchy subject. We know the Devil causes sickness. God doesn't. The first sermon I preached in 1995 at the beginning of our new church plant was about Solomon dedicating the temple. In the scriptural account, the glory of God came and the priests were unable to minister because of the heavy presence of God. His presence, or glory, is translated from the Hebrew word "kavod" or "kabod." Great word. You might want to look it up, if you haven't already. I expected, of course, the "kavod" to fall immediately following my inaugural sermon, as a sign of God's affirmation of our new church plant. It didn't. But this is why I'm telling you about that sermon right now. When the "kavod" touches me, which it does quite often now, the pain eases. That might give you a hint at what, or who, causes sickness.

Here's some more sickness experience. I've had two counterfeit strokes over the past 10 years. The enemy is adept at imitating illness. I'm not positive about this, so don't quote me, but if you agree with the deceit the Devil is peddling you might end up owning whatever the illness is. The best thing to do is to refuse to receive whatever it is, even if the malady is medically verifiable. I'm not talking denial, or "naming and claiming" it, I'm simply suggesting that refusing to receive illness is an excellent attitude to maintain.

Anyway, back to my "strokes" story. I discovered that doctors and nurses become extremely serious when there is an indication a patient might be having a stroke. And so they should. In my case, I was exhibiting various symptoms, such as vertigo and confusion. In the first episode, I underwent preliminary tests in the emergency ward, and was then discharged and instructed to return if symptoms worsened. Then I was sent home to suffer. A few years later, after the second episode, I was sent to the stroke clinic 30 miles south in Victoria. I spent the day there, while I underwent a comprehensive examination. The La-Z-Boy chairs were comfortable, and I nodded off a few times. The tests all came back normal. You tell me what was going on. All I know is I'm not going to agree with illness, especially since I'm the founding member of the Getting Younger Every Day Club.

That's right I forgot to tell you about my club. I founded the Getting Younger Every Day Club a few years ago. The club is growing, partly because there are no dues or mandatory meetings. There is only one suggestion. It's not a requirement for membership in the club, only a suggestion. And here it is. If someone during your day begins to complain about getting old and laments about all the challenges and ailments that plague the elderly, or they might even be younger and just complaining about life generally, you might respond to their complaints by saying, "Not me. I'm doing great, and I'm getting younger every day." But like I said, that's only a suggestion. Okay, so you might think the club is simply an excuse to sit around in the soft chairs in the coffee shop, solving the world's problems. And you might be right.

One Hebrew word for "glory" in the Old Testament is "kavod," and it means abundance, glory, and honor. It also has the connotation of weight, or heaviness. In the New Testament the Hebrew concept for glory (kavod) is translated into the Greek as "doxa." "Doxa" is the word for glory we find in the prayer of Jesus recorded in John 17.

We read in the book of Exodus that Moses wanted to see God's glory, his "kavod". We find the account in Exodus, chapter 33, verse 18:

"And he said, "Please, show me Your glory." Then He said, "I will make all My goodness pass before you, and I will proclaim the name of the Lord before you. I will be gracious to whom I will be gracious, and I will have compassion on whom I will have compassion." But He said, "You cannot see My face; for no man shall see Me, and live."And the Lord said, "Here is a place by Me, and you shall stand on the rock. So it shall be, while My glory passes by, that I will put you in the cleft of the rock, and will cover you with My hand while I pass by. Then I will take away My hand, and you shall see My back; but My face shall not be seen."

The word translated glory in this passage is "kavod". Today do we have the desire to say, as Moses did, "Lord show us your glory?" Do we want the glory of our Father God to increase in our midst? Do we want to glow with the visible light of God's presence, as Moses did, so that he had to cover his face? He was too scary for the people to look at. And he was so infused with the presence of God he remained in perfect health until he was 120-years-old, when God came to take him home.

Once in a while over the years, when I was being prayed for, a good intentioned person, when they realized no healing was forthcoming, would declare, "My grace is sufficient for you, my strength is made perfect in weakness." My thoughts on those occasions went roughly like this, "What inspired you to recite that scripture? Not God, I hope. God would not say that to me." But just the same time, I haven't been healed. Although, I do know that messengers of Satan don't enjoy the presence of the "kavod."

CHAPTER SIXTEEN

Another incident resulting from that 1990 Kansas City conference I told you about occurred in the late nineties when the well-known prophetic minister John Paul Jackson came to Victoria, BC. After one of the sessions, I asked him about a peculiar anomaly I observed when I saw him at that Kansas City conference. Each time I saw him his eyes seemed to have plates on them, like contact lenses, only they were visible. At the time I came to the conclusion I was discerning his seer's eyes, and the plates were essential to his prophetic gift. But when I asked him in Victoria about my observation at the Kansas City conference, he said the opposite was true. He said he had been under discipline at that time, and his seer's gift was effectively blinded. So what I had thought were his seer's eyes, were in fact his no-seer's eyes. Oh, well. He went on to say our fledgling church would in the future have a connection to Juneau, Alaska. The prophecy became a source of amusement to some of us, when we speculated on who would be the blessed ones in our congregation to be sent there. In 2013, my wife and I went for an Alaskan cruise. When we stopped off in Juneau I left my business card with a man who was preaching on the street. I thought it was the least I could do. I haven't heard anything yet.

CHAPTER SEVENTEEN

So how are you enjoying your journey through my life's highlights so far? I hope I'm not wasting your time. They say time is a terrible thing to waste, or is it a brain that's a terrible thing to waste? Either way we are all stuck here in time. When I wake up in the morning, I'm not only faced with the world's deceitful reality and its myths, I'm also living in time. I'm living here on earth in this time. There's no time in heaven. Have you ever tried to comprehend what heaven is like? And what do we, living here in time, look like from there? What's God's viewpoint? We know, of course, He tells us all about his viewpoint in his book, the one He wrote for us. And in his book He also encourages us to make the most of our time here on earth. So I find myself here every morning, waking up and living in time and hoping to make the most of it. I know, of course, in this life I can't live anywhere else but in time. So I am stuck in time, along with everyone else. I can't imagine not existing in time. Being outside of time is an alien concept to me. I can't imagine existing that way, but maybe you can. Think about it for a minute. No time. There's a word for living in "no time." The word is eternity. And eternity has no end. How weird is that? I can't imagine having an existence that has no end to it. But in heaven, even the concept of having an ending won't exist when I'm living there, where there is no time and no end to it either. But believe it or not, those who are born-again into the Kingdom of God, those who endure to the end here on earth, will exist in a place where there is no end. For eternity. That's hard to imagine. But it's the truth. It's the gospel truth. My existence will have another way of being, outside of time.

But, hold on a minute, not so fast, I'm not living there yet. I have this time here on earth to live in first. And the crucial question for those who live in this time, if they have ever heard the question, is what are they going to do about Jesus, the one who came to rescue us from time, the one who came to save people from the limits of time? Jesus Christ, Son of God, Son of Man, took the Son of Man to the Cross and resurrected him, and He is in the process of resurrecting His body, His body of believers. That means I need to redeem this time I'm living in now. And I'm to cultivate the truth of God's viewpoint in my life, as I'm making the most of my life here in this time. I need to convert my time to his service and deliver my time to him to fulfill his purpose for me. But at the same time, outside of this time we are living in, I'm seated in the Spirit with Jesus in the throne room. Ephesians 2:6 tells me that I am. God "raised us up together, and made us sit together in the heavenly places in Christ Jesus, that in the ages to come He might show the exceeding riches of His grace in His kindness toward us in Christ Jesus." And if that isn't wonderful enough, Jesus tells us where two or more believers are gathered in his name there He is in our midst.

So here I am. I'm here and there at the same time. In my body, I'm here in time and in the Spirit I'm there, where there is no time. But I only know I am here and there at the same time because I am living in time. In Ephesians 5:15, Paul writes, "See then that you walk circumspectly, not as fools but as wise, redeeming the time, because the days are evil." God created time for me and you to live in, and I need to make the most of it. How do I do that? I make the most of my time by having my priorities right and not running after the things of this world, the things of this time I am living in. I can have things, though, as long as they don't become idols. Nevertheless, all the things of this world are passing away. So while I am here, my main focus is to become more like Jesus, and learn how to love, and to be part of his body on earth in this time. And right now, at this time, I'm a new creation in Christ. And his new creation will, after the end of time, exist outside of time, where there will be no more death. Jesus destroyed death and brought life and immortality to light through the gospel. And since death is defeated there will no longer be any more "end of things" after the ages of earth are ended. There is an end to time, and then there is no time.

There is the millennial age, and then the end of the ages, and then the end of time. There has been some disagreement in theological circles about how the end of this age plays out and what happens after that, and I do mean in circles. But there's no sense getting into that. Right now, when I get up each day and

live my life in the world around me, I can't comprehend existence without time. Jesus entered into time
to rescue us from it. He paid the price for us to get out
of captivity to it, so we would no longer have to do
time. And while I'm here, I'm to redeem my time by
making the most of every opportunity. And I know
time is short. Everyone knows that. But on the other
hand God has a different perspective. With the Lord
a day is like a thousand years, and a thousand years
are like a day. In other words, when you are outside
of time, then time is all the same, a thousand years,
a day, same thing. Or to put it another way, because
eternity has no beginning and no end, then time as we
know it becomes irrelevant. But here right now I'm
living in this time, and so are you.

Do you sometimes pray for a perceived need and
then want to get an answer from God right now in
your timing? Have you ever done that? He might
answer you right now, or delay the answer for 30-
years? To us 30 years would seem like a long time.
Our Father in heaven doesn't see it that way, because
it's all the same. A day, 30 years, a thousand years,
it doesn't matter. God's timing isn't our timing. He
doesn't have a watch or a cell phone to run his life. He
is not running on our timetable. But at the same time,
where we are living, God has prepared a beginning and
an end for each one of us.

As I already mentioned, right now I am living in
both time and no-time. My human self is living in
time, but in the Spirit I am living in no-time. That is
why I can declare Jesus has already won the victory,

even though the end has not yet actually arrived. Jesus won the victory at the Cross. And I can also proclaim that I have won, because I am living in his victory even though He hasn't returned yet. So the end is all cinched up, and I can proclaim that fact confidently. I'm extremely happy about that. There's no doubt about it. And I know there is no doubt about it because I have read the end of the book, which He gave to me so I can see from his perspective outside of time. That's one reason why his book fits together perfectly. He knows the end from the beginning. So when I get up in the morning, I'm with Him and He is with me, with the victory having already been won. All I need to do is persevere to the end, and to make my journey's destination even more certain, Jesus is seated at the right hand of the Father cheering me on.

So why does it seem like life is hard most of the time? Easy answer. We are living in the world where evil persists, because the Devil persists. There is evil in this time we are living in. The evil-one is at work in this time, but at the end of time there will be no evil, and no evil-one to cause it. Apparently evil won't serve any purpose then. But in this time there is blatant evil, and also disguised, hidden evil. We are cautioned Ephesians in 5:15-16 to remember that fact: "See then that you walk circumspectly, not as fools but as wise, redeeming the time, because the days are evil."

Human history has chronicled the main activity of the human race. People fighting other people, with varying degrees of barbarity. Wars. And people not being able to govern themselves or get along. Competition and strife. That is what the world has been doing, but what about the Church? What is the Church, Christ's body, supposed to be like? How is the Church supposed to behave during this time? And how did evil get into the Church? The history of the Church reveals that most of the ills corrupting the world have also infected the Church. Jesus didn't die for a sick and splintered body, but for a pure and spotless bride.

Most people, if not everybody, need a lot of help to make it through their time here on earth. That tells me I need to help others, since people are living in the same time continuum I am. And people need all the help they can get. I am not here to compete against the others, or to get ahead of them, or to leave them in the dust. Because in this life time I am living in, there is really no other destination except to arrive at the end of time. And that fact begs the question, so where is everyone going, anyway? And since life can be a struggle in this time, I'm not supposed to judge others on how they are doing with their struggles, or be critical of who they seem to be. Instead, I am to look to myself and see how I am doing. Jesus tells me not to judge, or I will be judged. And there's that whole subject of sowing and reaping. I reap what I sow. Am I sowing to the Spirit for eternity, or am I sowing to the things of this earth? And how about you? What are you sowing to? Time will tell.

CHAPTER EIGHTEEN

I already mentioned John Wimber. He was the founder of the Vineyard movement in California. The Vineyard churches subsequently spread to other countries, and the movement became international. Wimber and the Vineyard had a profound impact on my life during the 80s. My connection with the Vineyard began in 1984, after I heard the news about a major outpouring of the Spirit there in Anaheim. I travelled south with a few other believers to see for myself if the reports were true. The Vineyard Church at that time was housed in a converted warehouse in Orange County. The conference we attended was called "Signs and Wonders and Church Growth." It was a major event. The manifest presence of the Holy Spirit of God was moving among us, and there were people being healed, and the new worship music coming from Wimber and the Vineyard was intense. I was on a tight budget in those days, and during the conference I lived mostly on Orange County navel oranges. At the same time I was extremely hungry for more of God, and I discovered that an orange fast can help you grow the Fruit of the Spirit. Sorry for that. During one ministry session I was being prayed for and prophesied over, and the heat in my body was extreme. I saw a vision of a youth movement on southern Vancouver Island, and then I saw young people flooding south into the Pacific Northwest. That hasn't happened yet.

In the late eighties, Wimber came for a conference in Burnaby, BC, a suburb of Vancouver. In one morning session he called for repentance among those who were gathered at Burnaby Christian Fellowship. The people gathered were mostly pastors and others in ministry. God was serious that morning. The ministers couldn't get to the floor fast enough, as chairs flew in all directions. It seems there was considerable sin in the camp, and the Spirit of God was convicting us all.

Wimber made several trips to Vancouver in those days. His last trip to Canada was in 1995. He spoke at a Vineyard conference in Kelowna, BC. He was sick. In 1993 he had been diagnosed with sinus cancer, and in 1995 he had a stroke, and in 1997 he had triple-by-pass heart surgery. When he was in Kelowna in 1995, he was squirting pig spit into his mouth to help him talk, since radiation for the sinus cancer had damaged his salivary glands. But his sense of humor was intact. At one point he said, "Half the people say the reason these afflictions have happened to me is because I was too easy on the prophetic movement. And the other half says the reason is because I was too hard on the prophetic movement." Later in 1997 he fell in his home and hit his head, causing a massive brain hemorrhage. He died on November 17th of that year. He was 63. His death was a sad event for the charismatic movement, but for him, as they say, it was all good.

CHAPTER NINETEEN

I worked in a bar before I was saved, and I also drove a taxi on and off. Whether I was tending bar or driving a taxi, people generally treated me as an anonymous person. In other words, working in those occupations people talk to you as if you are merely a sounding board, not a real person, just a bartender or a taxi driver. Incidentally, both jobs have the potential to provide excellent training for young people who want to be in ministry. It's the real world out there, and the people present you with their real life problems.

One night I drove a guy downtown to kill another guy. I didn't know I was doing that, of course, until later. On our trip to the murder scene he was extremely focused, ignoring me entirely. I was the anonymous taxi driver. I dropped him off at the back entrance of a downtown hotel and then drove around to see if I might pick up a fare at the front entrance. It wasn't long before a young couple came running out and jumped in. They were agitated and strangely elated. I pulled out into traffic and they told me a guy had come in and stabbed another guy once in the heart. No blood that way. I dropped them off at their destination and went straight to the police station. I knew immediately who had done the deed and thought I might as well give the police my trip-sheet particulars sooner than later. The detective who had just got the call was curious to know how I knew my fare was the assailant. The guy was really focused, I explained.

I was called to testify in the court case. When I was asked by the judge to point him out in the courtroom, my onetime taxi fare and I looked directly at each other. I was no longer anonymous. He got eight years for manslaughter. The killing was motivated by drugs and a woman. There was nothing funny about it.

Emotions can get you into trouble. So how are your emotions doing? No matter how you think they're doing, they are unreliable. Our human emotions in themselves have the potential to be completely unreliable and can lead us into committing serious errors in our lives. I suppose I could stop now and let you reflect on the decisions you have made in your life that haven't turned out so well, simply because they were based almost entirely on your emotions. And after you have thought about that for a while and realized the statement is in fact true then I suppose I could stop here. But instead, let's see if we can gain more insight into our emotions, insight that might be useful and helpful and might even prevent you from allowing your emotions to lead you astray in the future.

First, let's take a look at what we are made of. Scripture tells us we have three parts, spirit, soul, and body. 1Thessalonians 5:23 tells us, "Now may the God of peace Himself sanctify you completely; and may your whole spirit, soul, and body be preserved blameless at the coming of our Lord Jesus Christ." So here we are, having three parts. Most of us know our goal as believers in Christ is to have our minds and our wills line up with his. That process occurs as we allow him to clean us up through the sanctifying process of his word and his Holy Spirit. We apply the truth of scripture to our lives and allow his Holy Spirit to heal us, and help us, and guide us, so those things that interfere with our communion with God, the Father, are removed. So we, as believers in Christ, if we want to grow to maturity, are to be engaged in this sanctification process. Those whom God has chosen are chosen not only to be saved, but also to be sanctified. So far, so good. But what about our emotions? We know we all have emotions every day, in the same way we have thoughts every day. Also, our minds in agreement with our wills make decisions, often influenced by our emotions. But sometimes we have some thoughts and emotions that might be considered negative. Generally speaking, I think most of us are capable of recognizing the thoughts that are incompatible with what God tells us in scripture. And also we generally know when certain acts of our will are contrary to good judgment and God's will for our lives. But do we have the same kind of warning system when it comes to our emotions? We have some emotions we would term negative and others we would call positive. Although, there are emotions we might consider positive that can also mislead us. What we call positive emotions might, in fact, be even more deceptive. So we might want to consider that our emotions might be a little trickier, a little sneakier, than we realize. And could it be we have developed a habit of justifying our behavior when it comes to our emotions? For instance, you might think you deserve to be angry because so-and-so did this or that. Or you deserve to be angry because so-and-so didn't do this or that. Or you deserve to be melancholy because your girlfriend forgot it was your first-week anniversary. Or how about, you're so sad today because your pride was stepped on by your boss, so you'll quit and try to find a job where your boss will be more sensitive to your feelings. Or, you're embarrassed because you don't have a vehicle, so you go into debt and buy a new Mercedes to impress people. Or how about, because you didn't get your own way, you're justified in sulking and giving people the silent treatment. And so on. Don't you think it would be helpful if we could blow the whistle on unhealthy emotions in our lives, the ones masquerading as legitimate?

We also might need to be aware that the enemy has often deceived us into believing our emotions are justified in certain situations, when in fact the opposite is true. And the enemy tempts us to live there, in an unstable emotional state, believing we are totally justified in ourselves. We know, of course, some of us are more emotional than others. And some of us handle our emotions better than others. And, of course, we need to recognize that some of us have had serious emotional damage in our lives, requiring some serious, in-depth counseling and healing. There's no ignoring that. But quite apart from those kinds of emotional dysfunction, we can often give our emotions a free ride, and not identify them as a problem that needs to be addressed. In other words, do we let certain un-Godly emotions have reign in our lives, and then do we justify them because, after all, they are our emotions, so they must be right, because they feel so right?

We can usually recognize un-Godly thoughts, and we know when we are engaged in sinful acts of our will, but do we recognize destructive emotions that might be plaguing our lives? The earthly nature of human beings apart from divine influence is prone to sin and opposed to God. We are a mishmash of thoughts and emotions that result in actions of our will concerning what to do with, and in, these bodies of ours, often in opposition to what the Spirit of God would have us be and do.

The Holy Spirit of God is the only true source of genuine love, joy, peace, patience, kindness, goodness, faithfulness, gentleness, and self-control. We can consider these fruit of the Spirit as the standard for us to live by. How do these attributes, these fruit of the Spirit, relate to our emotions? First, there's no place for anger or hate or fear in God's love. In God's peace there's no place for anger, or aggression, or for arguments, and certainly there's no place for war. In God's peace, chronic fighting with our spouse to defend our rights is not allowed to co-exist. Patience doesn't become frustrated because expectations aren't being met or people aren't behaving the way they should. Or maybe I'm angry because God isn't acting on my prayers fast enough, so I'm disappointed, and hurt, and sad. And kindness doesn't react harshly or have contempt for others when they are behaving badly or even hurting us. Goodness doesn't lash out and degrade others when they oppose us. Faithfulness doesn't envy others but remains steadfast in character and doesn't despair. Gentleness isn't alarmed and doesn't panic and doesn't retaliate when attacked but offers a soft answer. And self-control doesn't agree with doing whatever feels good and says no to destructive emotions, which can cause hurt and division in our workplace, among families, and in congregations. In short, when emotions dominate our lives, relationships can become a mess.

Also, we might want to examine whether or not our human compassion is in alignment with God's heart and his compassion. We can have human compassion for people and groups of people, when what we are experiencing is simply our human compassion and is misplaced. We might watch a TV show and feel compassion for the poor misunderstood people in organized crime who are selling drugs and killing one another. And then we might buy an advertiser's product we see during a commercial that plays on our human emotions, to induce us to buy what they're selling. On the other hand, when our human compassion begins to agree more with God's compassion, then we are growing in the Spirit.

And while we are on the subject of emotions we might as well address the state of overblown romantic love encouraged by literature and Hollywood.

There is nothing wrong with the emotions that go hand in hand with the mating process, but the perversion of it, the over-glorifying of it, can cause unhealthy, unreasonable, and unrealistic expectations that often lead to disillusionment and divorce, once the rosy glow has faded. That is, when the two lovers discover their spouse is a person with imperfections, and surprise, surprise, is also inclined to argue about money. But on a positive note, once the discovery has been made that the other person is only human, then there exists the potential for both people to continue to grow in a loving relationship, as long as they are both dedicated in their journey to become more and more secure and established in the love of God.

So here it is again. Our human emotions in themselves have the potential to be completely unreliable, which can lead us into making serious errors of judgment in our lives. But there is help for us. God's love is the true emotion. In his love, in His true emotion, we can find the healing of our emotions. Then we can trust our emotions because they will then originate in the one true emotion, God's love.

Our emotional lives are intended to flow out from God's love, the true emotion. Our minds can think about God's love, and admire God's love, and study about God's love. Our wills can turn our being toward God's love by studying his word and praying to him. But our emotions experience God's love. God created emotions. God is an emotional person. God drew us to himself by his love. Love is emotion. Jesus wept, that's emotion. The Holy Spirit of God can be grieved, and He makes intercession for us in groanings that cannot be uttered. That's emotion.

I still remember dreaming the wordless groans a few years ago. I had the dream a few months after I came back from my trip to Israel. In the dream I am standing in a narrow street in Jerusalem. The street is stone and the high walls are stone. There's lot of stone in the Middle East. And in the dream I'm looking down the street and up at the sky toward the end of the street. I could see light there, contrasting with the dark street. The light might have been coming from the sun behind the clouds, or the light might have stood for the glory of God, or for the coming of the Messiah, but I knew it was the future, and that I would be going that way toward the light or the light would be coming toward me. But whatever was going to happen, I didn't want to miss it. That's when the heart wrenching and gut wrenching took place. I experienced in the dream a painful ache. And I was interceding for what? I didn't know, but it was about the future. The Holy Spirit knew, and He was groaning through me. And it was intense.

We need to have our emotions, saturated in God's love, flowing out to others. How do we do that? We can ask God to change us in the power of his Spirit, so we can be released from unhealthy emotions that are causing unneeded stress in our lives and in the lives of others. There is hope, when we volunteer to have the Holy Spirit heal us, so our emotions, and our minds, and our wills are in agreement with him. Then we will be living in his love. The one true emotion.

CHAPTER TWENTY

Now let's go back again to 1984. Bill Saunders, my pastor at the time, and I went to visit a man who was in the hospital in Victoria. He was in the intensive care unit awaiting a heart operation. He was a local business man and more than a little rough around the edges. His use of four-letter friend-getters was in-genious. He was skilled at salting them between com-pound words. But who was I to judge?

Anyway, we gained entrance to the ward and found him in his bed sitting up. After a few pleasantries, we asked if we could pray for him. He agreed with-out any expletives added, and I was surprised to see him extend his hands and rest them on his lap in the perfect receiving-of-prayer pose. I wondered where he learned that. Then we began to pray, and as I was praying in the Spirit an odd event happened. It didn't register on me at the time. During our prayer, his heart machine was flat-lining, and paper was spitting out of it. But as I was praying those facts didn't occur to me as significant. After a few minutes we stopped praying, and the machine let us know his heart had started beating again. It seems God had given him a spiritual heart operation. They went ahead with his surgery, and the operation was a success. He lived a few years after that, and I was told he later gave his life to the Lord before he died. One of the amazing details of the event was the fact that the nurses at their monitoring station in the intensive care unit hadn't come running when his heart stopped. The alarm should have gone off, but it didn't. I guess the Spirit of God didn't think the nurses were required to assist in a spiritual operation.

CHAPTER TWENTY-ONE

When a believer in Christ dies, we often say he or she went home. We know that our earthly home, where we are living now, is only temporary. At the same time believers are also living in the Kingdom of God, since Jesus is our King. But the Kingdom of God is a difficult place to imagine. To help me live there, I try to imagine the Kingdom of God as my home. A home is a much easier place to imagine. People generally have a yearning to be home, to be where their hearts are at rest, resting in the peace of a loving home. The journey home is also a theme in literature, dating as far back as the Odyssey, first written in about 800 B.C.

Humans have an inherent ache in their hearts to be home. When I pray the Lord's Prayer and come to the words "thy Kingdom come" I try to imagine Jesus bringing my true home here to earth for eternity. In the meantime, I am here living at home with Jesus in my heart. Jesus is with me, He is within me, and when I am with other believers, He is in our midst. His Holy Spirit dwells within me. I am at home. My home, the home in which my heart wants to live, is with me now. When I wake up in the morning I know I am living in his Kingdom. My heart is at home with Him. My heart has found a home; my heart is at home right now. Where is yours? The Kingdom of God is also our eternal home. That means I can relax. And when I go into the world I take home with me. Out there in the world I meet people who are also looking for home. I recognize them, because I see the hunger for home in their hearts, too. Then I have the opportunity to represent home to them and tell them about home. And then the offer of home is extended to others and established in the world. Then eternal home dwellers can congregate in God's house and read about home and talk about home and take direction from the Holy Spirit, who is at home with them. There they can be equipped to be more effective in taking everyone's true home out there to the world.

There are also those who have run away from home. They are most often called prodigals. They have run away from home for one reason or another. One common reason for their running away is they didn't find home welcoming or desirable. The siblings might have been continually fighting in the house and they just wanted to get out of there and live elsewhere. Or maybe the Spirit of God wasn't welcome in the house, so they felt there was something missing. It didn't feel like a real home. Or maybe they were tired of waiting for a move of God to happen, and they just couldn't wait any longer. So they ran away.

Waiting isn't easy. Waiting on the Lord can be hard to do. But I can wait in the comfort of home, waiting for direction from God, who is eternal and sees from an eternal perspective, so when I have eternity in mind, my waiting takes on a new perspective, his perspective. And at the same time I can focus on getting to know my Creator more and more and discover how I can best serve Him, since He is the head of the house. That means I am his son serving in his house. I am waiting on Him. The Hebrew word for "wait" in the Old Testament stresses "the straining of the mind in a certain direction with an expectant attitude, a forward look with assurance." Many ministry leaders seem to think it's easier to do their own Kingdom building, instead of waiting on God and hearing his voice. Our western culture does not major on waiting. The urgency of getting what I want right now permeates western culture. There are forces in the world system insisting I become a slave to it. And there's no end in sight, unless I stop and decide to live in God's system. Unless I stop and realize I am living in the Kingdom of God, where I am living confidently and securely at home. I need to be freed from the worldly thinking that promotes debt, and be free to live in God's Kingdom, where everything I need is free. That is God's economy. At the same time, what I really need is love, and love is free in the Kingdom of God. Love for God and for one another, it's free. People only want to be loved. When I am living in the Kingdom of God my basic needs are being met. I'm safe and secure at home. And as a bonus, my Father in heaven doesn't mind that I'm still living at home, where He is paying all the bills. And at home my need for significance and security are also met. I am significant in God's eyes, and I am secure for eternity. I am also significant, because of the gifts and talents He has given me to serve him and others. And when I'm living in a community of true believers in Christ, my security and significance increase, as the love of God grows in our midst.

To be established in my true home, I need to eliminate from my heart the world's view of things and replace my earthly perspective with a view from the Kingdom of God. When I am seeing from God's view of who and where I am, then I am able to wait, since I have nothing to prove. I have no Kingdom to build for myself, because I am already living in one, my Savior's. And I am at home.

CHAPTER TWENTY-TWO

That conference I already mentioned, the one I went to in 1990 in Kansas City was held at the Municipal Auditorium. Most of the prophetic-movement notables were there, including Bob Jones, Paul Cain, Rick Joyner, Mahesh Chavda, James Goll, Mike Bickle, John Paul Jackson, and a few others, including Vineyard founder John Wimber, who had come to discipline the Kansas City prophets. They had been accused of prophetic inaccuracy. But that's a long story, and this isn't intended to be a history. That whole prophetic scene at the time isn't my highlight. This is: The Canadians attending the conference were called to a lunch meeting to talk it all over. During the meeting I repeatedly saw the image in my mind of Niagara Falls. At a subsequent meeting, I asked one of the elders what he thought of my vision. He said God would show me in time. God did. Marc Dupont, a Vineyard pastor from San Diego, gave a prophecy in 1992 that an immense wall of water like Niagara Falls would wash over Toronto in late 1993 or early 1994, launching a global spiritual revival. On Jan. 20, 1994, 18 months later, it did, and I was eager to see in person what was happening there.

In November 1994, I went to the Toronto Airport Vineyard for a conference. I went not having a place to stay because I was on a tight budget. I couldn't afford to pay for a hotel room by myself and also eat. My plan was to go to the conference site to see if there was anyone on the bulletin board wanting to share a room. As it turned out there was a note posted by a man looking for someone to share with. I don't remember what the administrative logistics were, but I arranged to meet him in the lobby of a nearby hotel. But it didn't seem very nearby, since I was on foot and pulling a suitcase behind me. I eventually found the hotel, and it was a high-end establishment. I decided to go in anyway and sit in the lobby. As I was sitting there I began to complain in my mind. I'm thinking that this hotel is expensive, and if I split the expense of a room, I still won't be able to eat. So wasn't that just fine. I came to this conference, suffer most of the day, and now I also have to fast, too. Nice. And to top it all off, the scripture comes to my mind, "endure hardship like a good soldier of Christ Jesus." Well, I was tired of enduring hardship, and as for fasting, I told the Lord I simply didn't feel like it right now.

I continued to sit and complain to God, until a man in his thirties came in, and I just knew it was him, because he was dressed like an Inuit, but he wasn't one. We met, and it turned out he was an American from the southern states dressed for the weather in Canada. I pretended not to notice. We exchanged pleasantries and then headed for the room. On the way up in the elevator, I asked the big question, "How much is the room?" He said, "Oh, don't worry about that, my church paid for it, and it's got two double beds, you can have one of them."

Yay, wow, I thought, and I'd be able to eat, too. We got settled in the room, and later I suggested we go out for something to eat before the evening session. I was feeling generous, so I told him I would buy, since he was giving me a free bed. But he said, "No, that's okay, I'm going to stay here and read. I'm fasting."

There's a lot that can be said about the fasting discipline. Jesus said, "Moreover, when you fast, do not be like the hypocrites, with a sad countenance. For they disfigure their faces that they may appear to men to be fasting. Assuredly, I say to you, they have their reward. But you, when you fast, anoint your head and wash your face, so that you do not appear to men to be fasting, but to your Father who is in the secret place; and your Father who sees in secret will reward you openly." Matthew 6:16-18

I don't want to lose my reward, so I'm not going to tell you anything about my fasting experience. But if you would like to read an insightful account of an extended fast, I recommend, *Bye Bye Bertie*, Quotidian Books, 2010.

CHAPTER TWENTY-THREE

How hungry are you? I don't mean is your stomach growling? I'm asking you about a more essential hunger. We all know we have a hunger for food to fill our stomachs and provide nourishment for our bodies. But how much hunger do we have for the spiritual realm? One hunger is physical, the other is spiritual. For our eternal well-being spiritual hunger is more essential. Have you ever ached, hungering to be in a deeper relationship with your Creator? I get the ache sometimes, and I feel undone. Isaiah was undone when he saw the Lord.

Of course, we can choose to ignore our need to be in a close relationship with our Creator. We have free will. Or we might fill our need with other things. That's what most people do when they don't want to face the fact they were created, and there is a God, and Jesus came to save them. They try to feed their need with whatever else they can find that enables them to continue ignoring God. In our country, people don't go hungry. We might be late for a meal, or miss a meal, and then we say we are hungry. Most of us do have an idea of what hunger is, if only in a superficial way. But most of us have never really been starving, though we might have said we're starving after having not eaten for a few hours, just to be dramatic. But what about spiritual hunger? How important is spiritual hunger to us? Do we even want to be hungry for God?

I think we know what happens when we ignore God and don't go to him for spiritual nourishment. Usually what happens is our spiritual lives shrivel up and die. And for those who have never known the Lord, the longer they live without a true spiritual connection to God the harder it is for the truth to break through to them. That's because they have let themselves be controlled by various forces in the world and have spent their lives feeding on so many other things that they are insulated from the truth. But I think it is safe to say there is a spiritual hunger in human beings that should not be ignored or neglected. Our most essential hunger, whether we are aware of it or not or even want to be aware of it, is spiritual hunger. Why is that? Because we were made that way. Of course, there will always be those people in the world who will refuse to respond to the one true God and will never come to him for spiritual sustenance. They will be content to feed on other things. But if spiritual hunger is not in our lives, then it should be, because it is essential for our lives and for our well-being. Jesus tells us those who hunger and thirst for righteousness are blessed, for they will be filled.

You probably have read about Jesus feeding the five thousand by the Sea of Galilee. Five small barley loaves and two small fish were multiplied to feed them all, and afterward they collected twelve baskets-full of the pieces remaining from the five barley loaves. The people who witnessed the multiplication of the bread and fish were impressed. Later they went looking for Jesus. When they found him he told them why they were looking for him. Jesus knew their hearts and told them the real reason they were looking for him. They were looking for him not because of the signs He performed but because they ate the loaves and had their fill. They weren't looking for him because He performed the sign of feeding the five thousand. They were looking for Jesus because they had been fed; they were looking for him because their stomachs were filled. They were looking for more food and, no doubt, wanted to discover how they might get more. And if you continue with that line of thought, you might come to the conclusion that they saw Jesus as a great source of provision, and perhaps a great source of profit, also. Imagine if they themselves had the ability to multiply enough food to feed five thousand people. That's a lot of food, enough to feed a whole town. Estimating the cost at about $5 per meal, which would be cheap by today's standards, a total of at least $25,000 was produced out of thin air. What they wanted was the food, and maybe the financial benefits such a supply might bring. They were not so interested at this point in the actual provider of the food. But Jesus tried to set them straight. He told them they had their priorities wrong, and then He told them what they should be seeking. He told them to change their focus from natural food to true spiritual food. But they continued asking him how they might produce food out of nothing. They wanted to multiply bread. But Jesus told them it wasn't food in this life they should be seeking. Their lives were not to be centered on what they might do, even if they could perform miraculous signs and create bread. What was essential to their lives was the One in whom they were to believe. They were to believe Jesus is the Son of God, the one our Father in Heaven sent to them. But they continued to tempt him. They wanted him to make more bread and fish for dinner. They wanted him to give them more physical evidence to prove to them He was sent from God, and maybe get something more to eat in the process, and maybe learn how He made the food multiply. And really they were not too interested in who He was. They were asking him to give them a never-ending bread supply to sustain them in this life. But then Jesus became even more direct. He told them He was the true source of life. He was the spiritual bread that would feed them. Jesus was standing in front of them, not just as their earthly provider but also as their eternal provision. Jesus told them He was the source of eternal life, and they needed to come to him and believe in him. So they needed to answer a question. Were they hungry for bread, or were they hungry for God? We might ask ourselves that same question today. Jesus says if you are hungry for God, here I am with you now. Do you want me? Loaves of bread are temporary. Anything we might hunger for in this life is temporary and simply a substitute for the real thing. Believing in the Son of God is eternal.

Then the Jews began to grumble. How much grumbling do we do when our physical needs aren't met? The Jews who were grumbling could only see Jesus in the physical realm. They saw Jesus, the man who had a father and mother, not Jesus, the Son of God. They were mired in their natural understanding. Jesus told them to stop grumbling, and then took them a step further. He told them if they ate his flesh they would not die, but live forever. But they didn't understand; they were still locked in their human way of thinking. Then Jesus gave them the whole truth. They needed to eat his flesh and drink his blood, and they would have eternal life. Now that was really something to ponder, and discuss, and argue about.

I think if Jesus was here today, and we didn't know him as the Son of God, and if we didn't already know He was telling us spiritual truth, then we would have a real problem with what He was saying, too. People in the world today don't understand, either. So we might even want to ask ourselves the question. Do we believe Jesus is the Son of God? He isn't standing in front of each one of us right now, but we have his word in his book, and we have his Holy Spirit. Do we recognize him? The Jews didn't realize that the Son of God was talking to them, and they didn't know what He was talking to them about. Do we? If we do know, then do we have a deep hunger for more of him? They must have known He wasn't telling them they needed to eat his actual flesh and drink his blood. Didn't they know that? They must have known that. Even so they didn't understand what He was saying, and they didn't know who He was, either. And they didn't understand that they would only have life when they believed He was God's son. And they certainly didn't understand Jesus was telling them that they would only have life through his death, that they would only have eternal life through the sacrifice of his body and blood.

Jesus is true life. Our earthly life sustained by food and water is only temporary. We might want to ask the question. Why would we hunger for anything in this life more than we hunger to be fed by real food, spiritual food, the spiritual food Jesus Christ provides for us? His disciples didn't understand, either. And then He told them the Spirit is the one who gives life; the flesh counts for nothing. The words He spoke to them were full of the Spirit and life. In the Book of John, the truth is written in black and white for us to read and understand. The Spirit of God gives life; the flesh counts for nothing. The words of Jesus are full of Spirit and life. The Spirit of God gives life, not the flesh that is temporary. Real life is in Christ. He will sustain us. When we have internalized that absolute fact, then material things, and provisions for this life, become minor concerns. Then our hunger is directed toward our Father in Heaven and our true home. Earthly bread then takes second place.

If we do want to gain insight into our true motives in this life, fasting will provide it. When we fast we are putting food in second place. Fasting says to God and to ourselves and to the spiritual realm we are putting our spiritual hunger for more of God ahead of our natural hunger for food. Fasting gets to the crux of the matter in a hurry. Blessed are those who hunger and thirst for righteousness, for they will be filled. Jesus is our righteousness and He will fill us. The words of Jesus are full of the Spirit of God and of life. The word of God is alive and active. The word of God will change us.

Many of his disciples left him then, but Simon Peter said he and the true disciples didn't have anywhere else to go, since Jesus had the words of eternal life. Peter confessed they had come to believe and to know that Jesus is the Holy One of God. He understood. Peter knew there was nowhere else to go except with Jesus and then on to eternal life in him.

How about you? How much do you want God? How much do you want Jesus when measured against filling yourselves with the things of this world? We know natural food is life; without food we die. But Jesus is the bread of true spiritual life, and without him we die. Our sustenance in this life needs to be in him. We need to be hungering for more of him. I think we all know the feeling of being hungry. We need to cultivate that same kind of spiritual hunger for him. And we can ask him for it. And we can pray for others to get it, too.

Hunger comes from God. We can't pump it up. The more we seek him, the more we will know him, and knowing him more will cause our hunger to increase. I don't think we can be too hungry for more of him. And that ache I get from time to time? It is a pleasant hunger that continues to be satisfied.

CHAPTER TWENTY-FOUR

Now back to that 1994 conference in Toronto. On the Friday night, after the evening session, I was sitting in the lobby of the hotel again, and a group came out of the bar, three young men and a woman, all in their early 30s. And they were planning to call a cab, but in the meantime they sat down to collect themselves. Their party night seemed to be over. They had been drinking, but they were relatively sober. And unhappy. I overheard them talking about the state of the world and how lousy it was, and so I saw my opportunity to join the conversation, which I did. We had a friendly discussion. They were even willing to listen to my point of view. When the discussion seemed to be over, one of them called a cab. As they were getting up to wait outside for the cab, I asked one of them, the one who was the most vocal and seemed to be the most interested in the gospel, if I could pray for him. I'll call him Bob. Bob said, okay, with a *why not?* sort of attitude, so I began to raise my hand to pray. Before I could get my arm up, the power of God hit him, his eyes snapped shut and he fell over backwards. Another believer from the conference, who had been eaves-dropping on our conversation, ran over behind Bob, just in time for Bob's head to hit his shin, and there Bob was, on the floor, his head propped up on my new assistant's shin.

What now? Bob's friends were looking at each other, eyes popping, wondering what was going on. I looked across the large lobby toward the desk, and the clerk seemed fairly interested in what was going on. He started heading our way. He came and looked at Bob, and announced, "I'm calling an ambulance." I said, "No, he's alright, he's just, uhh...he's uhh...he doesn't need an ambulance." The desk clerk looked at me, shrugged, and then said okay. He started to head back to the desk, but half way there he changed his mind, turned around, and headed back toward us again. He looked at Bob, and said, "No, I'm calling an ambulance." And away he went.

In the meantime, Bob started to come around, and his friends helped him up, as their cab arrived. They then began to shuffle toward the revolving door with their friend. The only thing I could think of to say to them as they headed for the door was, "Do you want to wait a few minutes, and I'll pray for you, too." They were polite, but in a hurry to leave, said, eyes wide, "No, that's okay." Then they tossed Bob into the back seat of the cab, and away they went into the night.

So what purpose did all that serve, you might ask? I'll suggest that Bob and his friends had a lot to think about later concerning our discussion and the power of God landing on Bob. My guess is that God had Bob on a journey to come to Him, and this was a significant event along the way.

CHAPTER TWENTY-FIVE

In the early nineties a woman phoned and wanted prayer because she had to go to Vancouver and have an operation to remove a growth near her spine. The doctors said there was a significant chance the operation would leave her partially paralyzed and in a wheelchair. She was in an anxious state. Pastor Bill Saunders and I prayed for her, and she went to Vancouver for the operation. She came back in excellent condition. She told us she had gone for the surgery, and when they examined her prior to the operation the growth was still there, but when they operated they discovered the growth had turned to mush, and they only needed to suction out the remains and sew her up. She told us the experience resulted in her being an excellent witness to the doctors and the nurses in the hospital.

CHAPTER TWENTY-SIX

How would you like to hear the essence of a Sunday morning message I gave in the year 2000 that reduced our congregation by two-thirds? It seemed like the thing to do at the time. Give the message, I mean. Have you ever heard of the spirit of Jezebel? Ephesians 6:12 reads, "For we do not wrestle against flesh and blood, but against principalities, against powers, against the rulers of the darkness of this age, against spiritual hosts of wickedness in the heavenly places." Do people really believe that? Does the Church really believe our struggle is against those forces? The force of evil that reduced our congregation by two-thirds has been identified by the name Jezebel, after the Old Testament figure, Jezebel, who exhibited definable characteristics. This is the label used for this particular way the enemy uses to keep people captive. And the primary methods the spirit of Jezebel uses are manipulation, intimidation and control. A person who lives in this way is a victim of evil, and the people who are subsequently manipulated and controlled in this way are also its victims. It's important to note this is a spirit at work, and since it is a spirit at work it can influence both men and women to accomplish its goals. The name Jezebel is used to identify the work of this spirit, but the spirit, of course, is neither male nor female. In addition, Jezebel is identified with witchcraft, and we know from reading Galatians 5:19 that witchcraft is a work of the flesh, "Now the works of the flesh are evident, which are: adultery, fornication, uncleanness, lewdness, idolatry, sorcery (witchcraft)...." In other words, witchcraft is also soul power. And souls are powerful. But soul power can also be aided by the demonic realm and its evil agenda.

We can find an account of Jezebel's schemes in 1st Kings, chapters 18 and 19. Jezebel the wife of King Ahab has been massacring the prophets of the Lord, so in a dramatic showdown the prophet Elijah retaliates by slaughtering 450 prophets of Baal. Then Ahab tells Jezebel everything Elijah has done and how he has killed all the prophets with the sword. Then Jezebel sends a messenger to Elijah saying, "May the Gods deal with me, be it ever so severely, if by this time tomorrow I do not make your life like that of one of them." Elijah was afraid and ran for his life.

At the time of Elijah's greatest victory, we see that Jezebel issues one threat and Elijah flees for his life. I think we can understand the incredible evil power at work, which causes the prophet of God, who has just accomplished a great spiritual victory, to run from Jezebel in fear and discouragement. In other words, Jezebel swears to her Canaanite Gods, Astarte and Baal, and a powerful demonic force is released to send Elijah packing. Why was Elijah suddenly afraid for his life? This must not have simply been the threat of one woman. Darkness and evil, coming from spiritual wickedness in high places, overwhelmed him.

Also, we find a reference to Jezebel in the Book of Revelation, Chapter 2, where the Son of God is addressing the church in Thyatira: "I have a few things against you, because you allow that woman Jezebel, who calls herself a prophetess, to teach and seduce my servants to commit sexual immorality and eat things sacrificed to idols. And I gave her time to repent of her sexual immorality, and she did not repent. Indeed I will cast her into a sickbed, and those who commit adultery with her into great tribulation, unless they repent of their deeds. I will kill her children with death, and all the churches shall know that I am He who searches the minds and hearts. And I will give to each one of you according to your works."

We see that Jezebel is in the church and also in leadership. She teaches, and she has a following, since she misleads God's servants. She is self-promoted and has great ambition. She calls herself a prophet. She entertains lust, causing God's servants to commit sexual immorality. She is not teachable, since she refuses to repent. And those who commit adultery with her are headed for great tribulation, unless they repent. Her children will be killed. This is not a spirit anyone would want in the Church, or to have for a mother.

This spirit of manipulation and control influences the saints in varying degrees and can be found in the Church today. When it's found operating in the Church it is usually because legitimate spiritual authority has been weakened to allow this spirit to rule, in the same way Ahab, the legitimate King of Israel, was weakened to allow Jezebel to control him. It manifests in congregations where dominant members of church boards have manipulated and controlled pastors, and it has manifested in faithless pastors who have dominated congregations through manipulation and control. When true spiritual authority is put down, illegitimate authority rises up. Ahab was weak and easily manipulated and controlled by Jezebel. It goes without saying that this demonic spirit can have no real God-given authority of its own in the Church. And its goal, of course, is simply to destroy congregations.

As I was telling you, one Sunday morning in June, 2000, I gave the sermon exposing Jezebel. At the end of the message, I asked the congregation to stand and proclaim with me that the Jezebel spirit was now expelled and not allowed to remain in our spiritual territory, meaning City Gate Church. I soon learned afterward that when Jezebel is exposed and expelled it will cause as much trouble as possible on the way out, often taking people with it. By September two-thirds of the congregation had left. I doubt most of them really knew why. This spirit is allowed to infect the Church because most leaders instinctively know if they do confront it there is going to be major trouble. That's why the Ahab option is most often taken by the pastor. That way the pastor can continue to feed the kids and pay the mortgage.

CHAPTER TWENTY-SEVEN

I didn't tell you about getting lost in the back streets of Jerusalem, in the Old City. One night a group of us decided to walk from our hotel to the Wailing Wall. I enjoyed the walk and seeing the wall at night, but then I lost sight of the members of our group. That's when my trouble began. I thought I knew the general direction back to our hotel. I thought I did. A half-hour later I realized I didn't know where I was. Sure, I was in Jerusalem, in the Old City, but that's where my understanding ended. I continued to wander through the narrow, dark streets, which were more like alleys, really, with high walls on either side, until I found myself at the entrance to the Muslim sector. The men loitering there were not smiling and didn't appear sympathetic to my predicament. I retreated, as several other young men, lurking in a dark doorway, were producing sounds using some improvised device that, no doubt, were intended to simulate gunfire. I retreated in the direction I had come.

I seemed to be one of the few out for a stroll through the narrow passages at that time of night. I continued onward but began to realize this definitely was not a recommended tourist activity. A little while later, as I continued my attempt to escape from the dark and dingy Old City maze, I overtook a man who appeared safe and approachable. I asked him if he could help me find my way back to my hotel. He looked to be in his mid-fifties, tall, about 6-foot-4, with a wiry build. He stopped and put down his pack. He asked me if I knew my hotel's address. He then took a case out of his pack and opened it. Inside were his reading glasses. I handed him the hotel brochure I happened to have with me, and he examined it in the dim light. He returned his glasses to his pack, shouldered it and said, "Follow me."

On the way back to civilization, he asked me where I was from, and I told him. I asked him if he lived in Jerusalem, and he said no, he lived in Haifa. Once he had led me back to the main city streets with the lights and the traffic and the people, he said goodbye, and sauntered off.

I'm not saying he was an angel, but...

CHAPTER TWENTY-EIGHT

I didn't tell you about my eyes. I began wearing glasses for myopia when I was sixteen. My driver's license had the "corrective lenses" restriction on it. A few years ago, I was in a coffee shop, and suddenly the people I was sitting with became crystal clear. I wondered what was going on. As it turned out, my right eye had returned to 20/20. Since then my left eye has also been improving. Neither my family doctor nor my optometrist has an explanation for the change. When I was due to take my driver's test again, my right eye passed with flying colors, and so did my left. I no longer need to wear glasses when I drive. I can't say conclusively that God healed my eyes, but I'm seeing 20/20, nevertheless. I think I'm safe to say He had a hand in it.

How well can you see? The Kingdom of God is here. Can you see it? When He was here, Jesus said the Kingdom of God was among the people. The reason the Kingdom of God was among them is obvious to us now. The King was there with them. And He's still with us. He's with those who are born-again into his Kingdom. We can't see the Kingdom, but I think we can take his word for it. It's here. Can you see it now? When He comes again, the whole world will see him. His glory will light up the sky. But since we can't see his Kingdom, maybe we can try to remember we are living in it. Having spiritual eyes to see we are living in the Kingdom of God isn't just reserved for special believers. Seeing is for all of us. The Kingdom of God is at hand. Jesus came into the world bringing us the message of the coming of the Kingdom of God. He announced the truth that the Kingdom of God has come near to us, which means the Kingdom of God is here now. Jesus came and right here today where we are, we believers are inhabitants of the Kingdom of God, right now and on into eternity. Jesus is the King, and we are his people. Jesus also tells us, as I noted earlier, that God raised us up with Christ and seated us with him in the heavenly realms in Christ Jesus. How does it feel to be seated with Christ in the heavenly realms with our King? According to God's word, in the Spirit we believers are in heavenly realms with Jesus right now. His viewpoint is spiritual and eternal. Can you see? And we can ask the Lord to open our eyes to see from his eternal viewpoint. Not only that, but He tells us where two or three believers gather in his name, He's right here with us. He is with us right now and for eternity. His Kingdom is right now and for eternity. We are with him in the Spirit in heavenly places, and He is with us here right now. Both are true, because scripture says they are true. That means God says they are true. Good deal. Can you see? God's word is eternal. This isn't fanciful thinking or super seeing. We don't have to labor to try to see the truth. It's just the truth. It's just spiritual reality in the Kingdom of God. We might need to open our eyes to see that God's word is true.

Let's see what else we can see. God tells us He loves us. I think we can all agree with that truth, even if we don't experience his love every minute. It's just the truth. Even when things aren't going too well, we know God loves us. I think we can agree love is the atmosphere of the Kingdom of God. It has to be, because God is love. And dwelling in the Kingdom of God means we are saturated with God's love for us, even if we aren't aware of that truth every day. We might need to pay more attention and not allow the world out there to interfere. We shouldn't let the world threaten us and keep us fearful. There's no fear in the Kingdom of God. Fear can't live there. Love is the essence of our lives in the Kingdom of God. We are invited to live in his love, regardless of our circumstances in the world. We can invite his love to take over our lives. We can make an eternal agreement to give him our lives and to live in his love. He invites us to shed all that hinders our life in him. Unforgiveness and hatred aren't allowed. We live in the Kingdom of God, in his love, his peace, and his joy. We have an open invitation to dwell in the atmosphere of heaven. We don't need to bring anything to the party, either. Only our love for our Creator. Sounds perfect.

So what stops us from living in his love in the Kingdom of God? Do you think the reason is we really don't believe God's word? Or we might think his word seems to be kind of vague and doesn't really apply to the realities of life on earth. But the truth is that his word isn't vague and it does apply. Nevertheless, most days we don't really believe we are truly living in the Kingdom of God. Do we? Do you right now believe that? I mean do you really? Jesus says He has given us the Kingdom. It's ours to live in. But let's be real. I mean we all know the world out there works overtime to reinforce our unbelief. The world system has been established to oppose the Kingdom of God and God's love for us, his children. And the bottom line is that the bottom line runs the world system, not the love of God. The world out there doesn't love Jesus. That means the world system doesn't love his followers, either. Jesus told us that truth when He was here. I don't think we get up every morning to greet and confront the day and say, "Oh, I love the world system, I love the politicians and the financial system, because they love me so much, they're always working for my benefit, and they are taking good care of me." We don't say that, do we? Because it's not true.

For most people, living in the world is a struggle, a fight, especially if we are followers of Jesus, because the enemy hates us and wants to make our lives as miserable as possible. The Devil might let unbelievers have a good time for a while, just to lead them further into captivity, but his intended ending for them is misery. And, of course, the world has its own version of love. We are programmed to love our lives here in this world, to love the planet, to strive for world peace. And then, when peace is achieved, the brotherhood and sisterhood of humankind will be realized, as we sail into the future on the wings of a dove. And that's where and when in our earthly paradise true love will be found for us all on our happy planet, with all of us in love with Gaia and Gaia in love with us. All we need is love. That's an insidious, enormous lie.

John, the apostle, knew a lot about this subject, because he knew Jesus. He told us in one of his letters we are not to love the world or anything in it. He wrote we can't love the world if we love our Father in heaven. There's no room in our lives for both. And that same John wrote the Book of Revelation. He had an eternal perspective. He knew the truth. He knew the more we indulge ourselves in the world, the lower we descend into it.

So what do we spend our time seeing, you know, out there, and in our imaginations? Do we see ourselves in the Kingdom of God, or do we see ourselves chasing after the enticements of this life? What are we committed to? And how do we treat other believers who are also living in the Kingdom of God? What do we see in each other? Do we see one another through the lenses of our soul-lives? Or do we try to see the divine working of the Holy Spirit in one another, and focus on that? What do we want to focus on in each other? What do we want to see? If we want to remain spiritually blind then the enemy will oblige us, with the cooperation of our sinful natures.

So do we want to have our spiritual sight opened to understand spiritual realities? Or do we want to see the words of Jesus as words that we only try to understand with our intellect. Only words on a page. Or do we want to engage the words of Jesus with spiritual eyes and understanding? Just maybe we can ask for help in this. There is hope. After his crucifixion and resurrection, Jesus was with his disciples for 40 days opening the scriptures to them, and He taught them about the Kingdom of God. Of course we know they were Old Testament scriptures. They had to be. He opened their minds to understand what was written about him in the Law of Moses, the Prophets and the Psalms. We need to ask Jesus to open our minds, so we can understand the scriptures, so that the eyes of our spiritual understanding will be opened. And then we will be able to be active in opening the eyes of the blind around us. We need to receive the power to have our own blind eyes opened, our eyes that have been blinded from birth. We were blinded from birth, but when we were born again, Jesus gave us the opportunity to see clearly. And what are we hoping to see? Do we want to see with spiritual eyes? Are we going to see our eyes opened to the deception of reality television, and the Internet, and the news telling us, "This is the way it is?" Is it really? And our families who don't know Jesus, and those we meet daily who don't know Him, is this is the way they will remain? Will they really? The world sees believers in a certain way. But is their definition really us? Is that us really? But on the other hand how do we see ourselves? The way the world sees us or the way God does? Are we growing in the Lord from glory to glory, or are we descending into the world in ever-decreasing spirals. Jesus loves me. Does He really? Yes, He does. Jesus is the Truth, his Kingdom is the truth. We need to see ourselves walk-

ing in his light. The Kingdom of God is at hand.
   Open our eyes, Lord, that we might see.

CHAPTER TWENTY-NINE

On the flight back from Israel in 2017, we stopped in Frankfurt for the connecting flight back to Canada. When I arrived at the departure gate I noticed my boarding pass didn't have a seat number, and there was a long lineup. I thought there was a possibility I might get bumped, and I was tired. Then I heard my name being called. Oh, oh. I went to the counter and a smiling Lufthansa employee asked me if I would give up my seat. The worst had happened, I thought. Then he said, "And we will give you a seat by the exit door, plus 300 Euros." That was an offer I couldn't refuse. I didn't ask any questions, such as, "Why would you do that? Why would you give me a much better seat with plenty of leg room for the long trip home? And also give me 300 Euros?" No, I didn't ask that. There must have been a mix up, and I had no desire to un-mix it. Besides, I rationalized later, God must have arranged the blessing, and who was I to interfere? The flight was wonderful. I stretched out my legs and didn't witness to anyone.

I'm sure you've heard about money. Jesus said you can't serve both God and money. The Bible talks a lot about money. So does everybody. There are 1600 verses in scripture that have to do with money. And there are over 500 verses that include either the word money, or riches, or wealth. This is a sensitive topic, because the topic of money is tied to our fears. Scripture tells us the Devil holds us in bondage to the fear of death our whole lives. And most of us think money can keep us safe. Fear goes deep. We know money is something we need to survive in this world. Lack of money can cause fear and anxiety. We also know fear doesn't belong in the body of Christ. And we know fear can't exist in the Kingdom of God. Our security is to be found in the Kingdom of God, not in the kingdoms of this world. The world teaches us that money will keep us secure and prevent bad things from happening to us. Ultimately, that is a false security.

People often say money is the root of all evil. The fact is money isn't the root of all evil. The love of money is the root of all evil. Think about that. If we love money, then we have the root of evil in us. It's the Devil's root growing from a seed of self-preservation, or maybe from the desire to dominate others.

If we love money, we are not likely to be happy about giving it away. We don't like to give away something we love. But love it or not, God tells us to give it away. That's not exactly true. He tells us to give some of it back to him in order to kill the root. But Christians can be skilled at not doing that. Many Christians think giving their money for the work of the Kingdom of God is just like giving it away. It's their hard earned money, and they're not going to give it away. They just can't do it. It seems to be stuck to their fingers, and it won't let go. Others say they haven't got much money, so how can they give any? Good question. They're not likely to get any more, either. Like it or not, it's in our best interest now and eternally to give some of our money away. But it's not really giving it away, is it? It's giving it back, really. I mean, whose money is it really?

We spend most of our lives trying to acquire wealth to ensure our security. But we should know by now piling up wealth doesn't bring genuine security, although it can bring a false sense of security. It has to be a false sense of security, since there is no real security in money. There is only security in Jesus. There is only security in the Kingdom of God. Our identity is to be found in Jesus and in the Kingdom of God. Our identity isn't to be found in money. Our lives are not to be centered on what we have. In other words, money isn't what life is all about. Jesus is what life is all about. The Kingdom of God is what life is all about.

But we also live in the world, and the world has a system. It operates by trading. Those in the system trade for advantage, using the medium of currency, or of stocks, or bonds, or precious metals, or various goods. Also, the present world system trades in people's souls. People are slaves to it. In fact, actual slavery does exist. The buying and selling of people for various purposes, exists in the world today. It's the Devil's idea. There are also some who have chosen to literally sell their souls to the Devil. It's not fiction. It's not a movie plot. The Devil is a counterfeiter, so he offers people success and fame in exchange for their souls.

And we are all in the system, because the system is

in control of the world's economy. But it's not God's system. It's not the Kingdom of God's way of doing things. In the Kingdom of God it is our Father's desire to give us all things. God's system is not based on trading, it's based on giving. Jesus tells us to seek first the Kingdom of God and his righteousness and all the rest will be given to us. Hard to believe, isn't it? But that's God's system. We live in his Kingdom in his righteousness, and He takes care of us. He has given us our lives. Jesus has given us our eternal lives. We are saved by his grace. He now takes care of us in the context of the world system, because that's where we live. We are living in God's Kingdom, but the world and the Devil continue to affect our lives. The world system still tries to keep us captive, but that is the system we need to break free from. A major step in breaking free from the world system is being able to let go of a percentage of what we have earned through the world system and give it to God. When we give our money to God and the work of his Kingdom, we're converting ourselves and our finances from cursing to blessing, from the world system to the service of the Kingdom of God. In the process we are being released from our reliance on the world for our livelihood, for our existence. We are recognizing God as our source, who gives us all things. But our fears, and our doubts, and our lack of trust keep us bound in the world system, which has an economy that is hostile to believers in Jesus Christ. The world loves its own, but not Jesus, or us. But we do have the opportunity to convert the world system's money, by giving to God a portion of what we receive from that system. When we do that, we are saying God gave us the financial blessing, not the world. God gave us our jobs, not the world. God is taking care of us, not the world. The world system has no hold on us. We will take our hard earned money, and invest it in his Kingdom. When we do, we are proclaiming the system doesn't control us. The world system doesn't control our hearts.

We often think if we can pay off that last bill or that final debt, then we will live in financial freedom. For most people that never seems to happen. There is always something else that comes along to keep them in debt. As believers in Christ we might ask the question, "Why would God give us complete financial freedom, if our trust isn't in him to begin with, and if our lives are not in him? The question then becomes, if our trust isn't in God, if our hearts are not firmly committed to him, what would we do with our resources if we did have financial freedom? But when I give my money to God, I'm saying this money isn't what keeps me alive. This money isn't what sustains me financially. God does. Money doesn't control me. I think we need to understand that money is a deep, entrenched heart issue. Where is our trust going to be, in God, or in money? We can't serve both God and money. We know money is hard to let go of. But as hard as it is to let go of, that's how strong a grip it has on us. I think we know God doesn't need our money. In fact, He has instituted giving for our benefit, to reveal our hearts, to reveal where our true allegiance lies.

Then there are those who are undecided about giving, and they might try to test God by telling him they will be able to give when they have some extra to give. But unless they give a portion back to God right off the top, they are unlikely to let go of any at all. Those sticky fingers come into play, motivated by divided hearts. As for me, I'm going to give to God first. Why? Because all I have is his. And because I'm his, I don't want to have money controlling me. I don't want the world system controlling me. I'm giving God my heart and my money. Here is yours first, Lord. Money doesn't control my heart, you do. Giving is all about our need, not his. It's about our need for more of him, and his Kingdom, and to know how He does things, and how his economy works. And it's about our need to let go of our dependence on the world system, a system that's on the way out, a system that's based on the concept of "more."

We do need more, but it is God we need more of. As God's Kingdom is realized in us, and the world undergoes dramatic changes in the future, the importance of finances will fade into the background, compared to the enormity of what God is doing in our lives and in the world. As we become firmly established in God's Kingdom, our concern about money will come into proper perspective. So we might as well agree with God about this now and be set free from the bondage of money. For our own good.

Can we see how freeing God's plan would be for the Church? And can we see why there's always so much controversy about money, and why it's such a heart issue? The enemy works overtime to keep his system intact and to keep the Church captive to it. He stirs up the people in any way possible. He creates suspicion. He stirs up greed and distrust of leadership. And what about those TV evangelists? He keeps the pot stirred, and fogs the true issue, and keeps us from giving this huge part of our lives to God. God gives. The world system trades. The only way we as Christians can exist in the world system is by living in Jesus. Then He will provide a place in the system where we will be blessed, as we bring his Kingdom into the world, and as we convert the world's finances into provision for the advancement of his Kingdom. We are to do this through our obedience in following him and living in him. The world system will end; the Kingdom of God will prevail. There is a free inheritance waiting for those who follow Jesus. We would be wise to be set free from bondage now by observing God's commands about money. God is a big giver.

"The blessing of the Lord makes one rich, and He adds no sorrow with it." Proverbs 10:22

While we are on the money subject, have you ever wondered when, and if, you are supposed to give money to a person begging on the street, since we can almost guarantee where the money is going to go? I learned something about God's heart on the subject many years ago. An incident occurred at a local gas station and convenience store where I had stopped for gas. When I went inside to pay, a person was standing at the counter eyeing the cigarettes. It was Big Larry. Big Larry was called Big Larry because he was big. And every time he saw me he would ask for the usual handout. We had a history going back a few years, which I won't go into. Anyway, this time I decided I wasn't going to give him any money. After all, he would only buy cigarettes with it. I was justified in not giving it to him. So when he asked, I said no, paid for my gas, and left. A few steps outside the door a five dollar bill was lying on the pavement. The stern small voice said, "Now pick up the five dollars and go back in and give it to Big Larry."

The point of the story is we might want to listen to what the Holy Spirit is saying in situations where money is involved. We are only stewards of His resources, anyway. My judgments about Big Larry aren't relevant. God's heart is relevant. That doesn't mean we are to give money to anyone who is asking for it. We need only be attentive to what our Father in Heaven is saying about it at any given moment. A few years later I saw Big Larry in McDonald's. He came and sat with me, and I told him the story about finding the five dollars and the Spirit of God telling me to go back in and give it to him. Big Larry was blessed out of his holey socks when I told him.

Big Larry still asks for his standard amount when he sees me. Two dollars is usually all he wants. The price of a cup of coffee.

CHAPTER THIRTY

My other grandfather, not the pedophile one, was buried alive in the First World War. They dug him out. He endured many operations to correct how his insides had been rearranged. He was partly bald. The mustard gas had burned away his hair down to his pink and scarred scalp. I wrote a poem about him in my counterculture days. If you wanted to be a writer, then a book of poems was mandatory. Here's the poem, titled "Gramps":

> Beer sludge hanging over his belt
> Making the sidewalk move from side to side
> His soul buried alive in the Great War
> A scarred body groping home from the Legion
> Trying to remember something it forgot
> Or lost a long time ago

My grandfather would come to my Little League games after drinking beer in the Legion. I remember him standing on the hill above the first base line and in his booming, drunken voice yelling how bad I was playing, especially if I made an error. There was no one to stop him. My parents seldom came to the games. I remember bumping into my Little League coach about a dozen years later in a local bar. He invited me to sit down at his table. We talked about those Little League days. He remembered I had a lot of talent but seemed to lack confidence. He was being tactful. It wasn't his place to stop my grandfather's behavior, either.

It was surreal, drinking beer with my Little League coach in a bar, and he seemed sorry to see me there. It's funny sometimes, how life can turn out.

Maybe my grandfather's drunken yelling was his twisted way of expressing his pride in his grandson. Or maybe that's just my way of rationalizing his behavior. That said, his behavior didn't do much for my pride.

Pride, as you no doubt know, is a huge problem. There are proud people, mostly men, who would rather die with their boots on than acknowledge their Creator. "Dying with their boots on" means they would rather die while living their life as they have always lived it. They would rather maintain their prideful identity than give their lives to the one through whom they were created. I can still remember my first experience with this attitude. It must be 35-years ago now. I can see him lying in his hospital bed, dying of stomach cancer. "May I pray for you?" I asked, thinking I would pray for his healing. "No, I'm okay," he said. "Do you know Jesus?" I said. "No, I'm okay." "Anything I can do for you?" "No, I'm fine."

I still remember wondering at the time if he was wearing cowboy boots under the covers. Boots or no boots, he died a few days later.

About 15 years ago a man I knew from back in the '70s came into City Gate in the winter looking for dry socks. I'll call him Ben. He was a doctor's son.

Ben's father died and left him $2,000 a month. He had lots of friends at the end of each month. The alcohol flowed freely and the drugs were swallowed up or went up in smoke. His brains were scattered from over stimulation. His mind alternated between nonsense and near clarity. He had come into the church to see me because that morning he had been thrown out of the bootlegger's house. That's where he had been staying before his monthly allowance had run out. And now he was left out in the cold. For a few minutes his mind cleared, and I took the opportunity to present the gospel to him. He had heard it all before of course. And even though Ben was drowning at the bottom of the barrel, his pride wouldn't allow him to turn over his life, as dismal as it was, to his Creator. Pride. A person doesn't have to be rich and famous or gifted and talented to be prideful. Pride is at the heart of our fallen human condition. As for Ben, he put on his new socks and left. That summer I read in the local obituary section of the newspaper that Ben had died. He had been wandering in BC's interior and there had given up the ghost. Ben's obituary included the words, "He did it his way." The sentiment was intended I suppose to be his family's tribute to him and how he lived his life. What else could they say? He died in the summer, so he most likely wasn't wearing boots.

Pride is a hard one, a two-edged sword. I don't mean the kind of pride we might have in our work, or in a job well done, or the kind of pride we might take in those things God has created us to do. I mean the other kind, the fundamental kind, the deep-seated kind, the kind that sets itself up in rebellion against God. Pride is anti-God and anti-Christ. Pride is anti-Holy Spirit, since we are to be guided by him, not by our self-serving pride. I know that fact because the Devil fell for pride. And he is anti-God and anti God's children. So we can conclude pride is incompatible with the Kingdom of God. It has no place there. Pride can't be allowed to exist there. Pride only exists and is promoted among the kingdoms of this world.

In the Bible the words used that are translated from the Hebrew and Greek into our English word "pride" have the connotation of lifting oneself up above others, to exalt oneself. Pride manifests when people exalt themselves above others and try to create the illusion they have superior qualities, as they boast in their arrogance and worldly wisdom. But there are also those who are secretly lifting themselves up above others. That's the kind of hidden pride that might seem insignificant, since it's not being overtly displayed. But it's the kind of pride that damages the one who is captive to it, and sets them in opposition to God. Pride doesn't have to be obvious pride. It only has to exist. Secret pride that's hardly noticeable to others can often be running a person's life. The victim might even be so accustomed to it that they are kind and gracious to it, and accepting of it. They might even think it's who they are. After all, it's their self-image, their identity, and it needs to be defended, or they will lose their sense of self. But, in fact, that identity isn't them; instead it's a self-willed tyrant. Our true identity is in Christ. We are intended to be who He created us to be in him, and there is no pride in him. Almighty God isn't proud.

The prideful heart wants to be above everything and everyone else, and wants to make itself like God. That's what the serpent offered Adam and Eve in the Garden of Eden. And the lie was believed, and the world continues to believe the lie. The lie exists in the kingdoms of this world. But Jesus died to redeem us from the consequences of believing the lie, the lie that we can be as gods and live independently of our Creator. It's the pride of life. The pride of life on this earth. The truth is everyone on planet earth needs to decide who is going to be God in their lives. Their Creator or themselves? If a person has been told about Jesus, then there is a question they need to answer. That question is, "Who do you say Jesus is?" Of course, we believers in Christ, the "ekklesia," the called out ones, are living in the Kingdom of God, under the authority of the King. So the question should be settled. But is it? We might want to ask ourselves that question?

The Bible tells us living in pride opens us up to the Devil's lies. Pride is not allowed to exist in God's Kingdom. It was thrown out with Lucifer. We who belong to Jesus are to humble ourselves, which is an act of our will, and God will lift us up in due time. He will most likely lift us up, when we can handle being lifted up. When God lifts us up, it is not the same as lifting ourselves up. When God lifts us up we receive his favor, so we can complete the plan He has for our lives, not so we can be great heroes of the faith in our own eyes. Pride came into the world with the serpent, the deceiver. But when we are born again, and living in God's Kingdom, where pride is not allowed to exist, something has to give. We can't live authentic, fruitful lives in the Kingdom of God with our self-elevating pride intact. Rebellion and pride have no place in us, the redeemed, the "ekklesia," the called-out ones of God. If pride does find a place in our lives, God himself will resist us. When we are in a prideful state, God won't agree with us or with our great plans.

When we are in rebellion, God resists us. That's his nature. Our Father won't agree with our rebellion. Rebellion is not good for us. Why would He bless us in our pride? If He did, we would make a big mess of our lives and be unfruitful in his Kingdom.

When we, who have once committed ourselves to living in the Kingdom of God, continue to rebel, we come under God's discipline. His discipline can only be seen as his loving mercy, because God is love, and his discipline is for our benefit. And we might want to remember there is no place to hide. If we have ever thought about going back to the lives we led before we were saved, we might as well forget it. In fact there is really no place to go back to. The prodigals will discover that, sooner or later. Let's hope and pray they come to their senses, sooner rather than later.

When we were baptized, the truth is we left our rebellion under the water with our old nature, and we were raised a new creation. But in actual practice, our human pride often keeps bobbing up and doing the dead man's float in our lives. We know in our hearts we were created to worship God, not to worship ourselves, or one another, or great political leaders, or so-called great humanitarians, or gurus, or movie stars, or pop stars. We will never be happy or find fulfillment worshipping ourselves, or others. And that's what our rebellion boils down to. The desire to be worshipped. That is Satan's goal. He wants to be worshipped, and he wants us to follow his destructive example.

Pride is not the affliction of only those who by the world's standards are succeeding in this life. Some people might be living in a place of their own perceived inferiority, where they think they are no good, and that others are better, and they will never amount to anything, or everything was stacked against them, or bad things have happened to them. But what if they somehow were to escape such a sad and dire state? Their next destination, if their pride has not been dealt with, and they haven't given their lives to their Creator, will be to develop their own self-importance, and to let everyone know how they conquered adversity, and how others should admire their courage, as they continue to want their own way, not God's way for their lives. Of course, most people want to be self-directed. When we examine our motives, isn't that what we really want? Could it be we really want to have our own way, not God's way for us?

Lucifer was kicked out of heaven. And now he wants us to worship him instead of worshipping God.

So when we follow his prideful example we have taken up the cause of our adversary. We are not wise when we are aiding and abetting the Devil's plan to be worshipped. Maybe we think we can live in the Kingdom of God with our self-serving pride intact? Or maybe we don't even recognize our condition. Have we examined ourselves and asked God to help us to see? We need to surrender and put ourselves under God's authority in all things. In that position, under God's mighty hand, we won't continue to be proud. But when we live in our pride, we are food for the Devil's system, swallowed up by the enemy. That's not a very nice place to live, being slowly digested through the Devil's system.

We know we have a basic need to be loved, and that need is perverted if it's not the love of God we are seeking first. When we seek him and his Kingdom first, everything else follows along. In the Kingdom of God our Father loves us, and we are secure, so why would we want to lift ourselves up, or live anywhere else? For what reason? To challenge him and have our own way?

That's not a wise choice to make. Our Father is already taking care of us. When we are living in him we are having our needs met. That means living in pride-directed lives is pointless and useless, since we have nothing else to prove, and since we have already been approved by the King. We don't need to be lording it over others when God is in control of our lives.

When pride is dealt with, the potential exists for true community because the Holy Spirit, who dwells in us, is then free to lead. Then we will be living in an atmosphere that will allow us to become who we are, an atmosphere where we can be healed of our old selves, and where we will feel safe to repent and admit to one another we're not God. Community is a word we often hear in Church circles. How do we create community? Let's create some, maybe have a potluck. You know, get to know one another. If that's as far as it goes, then the community is headed for trouble. Pride needs to be dealt with, so that there is no competition among those who are serving various functions in the body. Then the walls we erect to protect us from having our not-so-nice stuff revealed will be lowered. Masks can then be removed. There will be no prideful image to defend. Then we can seek forgiveness, and get cleaned up, so we can be free in the Kingdom of God to be ourselves. And no one will be better than anyone else, because the world's way of determining worth will be done away with. First seek the Kingdom of God and all you need you will receive. As believers in Christ, I think most of us know by now that life in this world most likely won't get easier in the future. That means we need to be living as close as we can get to the King. That's wisdom, to do everything we can to get to know Jesus more. He is the one we need to get to know now, not a few years from now. It's urgent, it's always urgent, and He is waiting to hear from us.

Believers in Christ are a new creation, called to walk humbly in the power of God. We need to be aware of our true situation. We need to know who

God is, and we need to know who we created creatures are. When we see who God is, and who we are, then we are able to understand our situation, and to know that living in humility is the only way to go. But how do we discover who He is? We can discover who He is by absorbing his word and being guided by his Spirit and repenting of our worldly pride

Here's a further personal note on the subject of pride.

In 2014, I was shortlisted in The Word Guild's Contemporary Fiction category for my novel *The Darkest Valley*. The Word Guild awards are the Canadian equivalent of America's Christian Book Award. I flew to Toronto for the ceremony. I didn't win. Later, after consuming the juice and cookies, I walked the mile or so back to my hotel. Before I got there the heavens opened up. It wasn't a vision. It was more like a monsoon. My ceremony suit was soaked by the time I got back to the hotel, and my literary hopes were drowned, too. I hung my suit to dry on the shower curtain rod. I hung my disappointment in my mind beside all the others. My biggest writing disappointment was in 2005. That was when Broadman and Holman, now B&H Publishing Group, published my novel *Bye Bye Bertie*. The novel is a parody of 1940s detective novels and a satire of Christian behavior. It's also a farce. They printed 10,000 copies, mainly distributed through their LifeWay book store chain. A lot came back. B&H and I discovered the Christian community of readers didn't share my sense of humor. Parody, satire, farce did not sell well. I also had the second in the series ready to go. It never went.

I bring this sad subject up to give you some insight into the writer's heart. My heart. When *Bye Bye Bertie* was first published, I had expectations. They went like this. A successful writing career would free me from the painful, burdensome pastor position. It would be a legitimate escape. After all, I could continue ministering to people by writing Christian books. I could minister to people at a distance, thus eliminating the need to deal with people's life challenges face to face. And why not? I had served my time in the pastoral role, and it was time for me to move on. Can you hear God agreeing with me? I tried to get him to agree. I even tried ventriloquism. You know, throwing my silent voice and pretending it was Him. Have you ever tried that? But guess what? Fifteen years later I'm still serving in the pastoral role. I'm not saying God intentionally sabotaged *Bye Bye Bertie* by stifling his children's laughter, so that I would continue fulfilling his purpose for my life. I'm not saying that. I will say I was unhappy with Him for not allowing me to do it my way, and for not tickling His kids when they were reading my hilarious novel. Okay, so I was more than unhappy. But when I stopped pouting I realized He had exposed my heart. Who knows where a successful writing career would have taken me at that time in my life. Farther away from Him, most likely. Of course, I'm much more mature now. But when I say that, I don't mean to suggest you should promote this memoir to your friends, relatives, and acquaintances.

CHAPTER THIRTY-ONE

Now let's travel back in time to the early eighties, when I was introduced to the demonic realm. The first church I attended had a community outreach called The Freedom Center. I spent a lot of time there. It was a drop-in center, where we ministered to anyone who might drop in. Needs were met, and the gospel was preached. But after a couple of years, the Devil wiped it out, and it happened something like this:

A middle aged man in shirt sleeves came into the prayer room at the Freedom Center. He stood for a few seconds, staring at the ceiling, and then he sat down.

"My daughter told me last night about you," the man said.

"Your daughter? Who's your daughter?" I said.

"She lives in Victoria. She had a dream about the Controllers shutting things down."

He began rolling up his shirt sleeves to his elbows, as though he was preparing for something? His exposed forearms were red and raw. They were badly burned; either that or they were covered with severe eczema.

The man shook his head and said to the floor, "What, me? Oh, they have been contacting me for years now."

The man might have passed for the twin of the grandfather on the Munsters, except his face appeared to alter and shift, but not just his expression. His face's structure seemed to change.

The man said, "She saw it in a dream."

"Do you live there?" I asked.

"Sometimes," the man answered. "They know what's going on."

"What happened to your arms?" I said.

"It's resistance. I don't flow through exactly right."
Then the man's face did it again. It blurred and changed.

"How do you know that?" I asked.

"I'm an engineer."

He looked like he might just be an engineer. But what was he doing here? His dark gray pants were wool and tailored; he wore new black loafers, and his blue pin-striped shirt had a Pierre Cardin symbol on the pocket. So what was he doing in a drop-in centre, talking gibberish? He wasn't drunk. Drugs maybe, or insane?

He said, "You don't understand. Nobody does. The Controllers. They do it with beams and force fields and electrical impulses. See."

The man held out his arms.

He said, "Too much resistance. I'm being punished for my blockages. They beam down the punishment." He lifted his eyebrows toward the ceiling. "They're up there."

His face began to shift again. He then became

the Pope, like the model grandfather. A man you could relate to.

"Where do you work?" I said.

The man turned his head toward me, exuding the warmth and understanding of the Pope about to bless a peon.

"I'm resigned," he said.

He then shifted back into his Munster role.

"You haven't got a clue how it all works," he said.

"How does it work?"

"You know a bit. You're the straight-shooter. There are others that shoot straight, but you're a gun-slinger, okay? The Controllers do it," the man said and rubbed his forearm. "This is nothing."

"Where are they?" I said.

He tried to laugh at my ignorance but sputtered instead.

"You don't know," he said. "Arms are burning. Yes, I'm going, got to go. I know. Message is clear here. You got the message."

"How are they going to do it?"

He rose from the chair and said, "A secret naturally, but you know the way they always do. Fire. They always do that. The fire comes down. Shooting rays, you know, straight-shooter. Power coming down. You know. The straight-shooter has quit."

Did you make any sense out of that? Maybe not. Schizophrenia? I don't think so. The facial features of schizophrenics don't metamorphose, as far as I know. But whatever conclusion might be drawn, one fact remains. There was a fire ignited in the Freedom Centre that same night. And it wasn't a revival fire, either. The wood burning furnace somehow set the place alight. There was enough damage caused to the building to prevent our outreach ministry from continuing. That is what happened as the result of the man's visit, but in one's natural understanding of how reality works, it made no sense at all.

My conclusion: It is unwise to engage the demonized in friendly conversation and become fascinated by what the Devil is doing.

CHAPTER THIRTY-TWO

I think it was in 2012, or around then, when my wife and I were driving to the bank on a Sunday morning, prior to the service to do some necessary banking. We stopped at a light and were going to turn left on the street that led to the bank parking lot. I then noticed that a woman was coming from the mall on our right to turn left and drive up the lane beside us. That was all fine except she had a coffee in one hand, and she was looking back over her shoulder, at what I don't know. A problem was developing. She was going to turn into our lane instead of the one beside us. I could see she was bearing down on the centre of our front end, but then she looked like she was only going to collide with our left front end. And then time and space shifted somehow and instead of a collision, she went through our left front fender and continued on her way, driving up the lane beside us. And away she went. She couldn't have done that without supernatural assistance. If she had simply swerved to miss us at the last second, relying only on her own driving ability, she would have, at the least, gone past us, crossed two lanes, hopped the curb and smashed into a store front window. I would have liked to talk to her afterward, to hear her version of the event, but she was gone. When we were standing in the bank, waiting for an open ATM, our knees were shaking. An angel did something, and reality had changed, supernaturally.

I guess God didn't want us to miss the Sunday morning meeting.

CHAPTER THIRTY-THREE

I asked the question a few chapters ago, how hungry are we? I'll ask it again. If you have fasted for a few days you might have had a taste of what hunger is like. In many countries hunger is a way of life. Most of us in the West are privileged to have enough food. But generally we are starving in another way. If we are not feeding ourselves spiritually, then we are wasting away. We need natural food to grow. We need spiritual food to grow. If we are not living in the truth our growth is stunted. If we don't know the truth, then we are spiritually starving. The word of God tells us the Kingdom of God is within us, or at hand, or in our midst. But most of the time we don't seem to be aware of it. How is that possible? Scripture tells us that believers in Christ are in the Kingdom of God. But is the Kingdom of God where we really want to be? Do we want to live in close relationship with our King? Also, scripture tells us the Holy Spirit is within believers in Christ. He's in us, but do we know him very well, if at all? So, how can that be? And if, in fact, we hardly know him, we would want to keep him away from our sensitive areas. Why would we let a virtual stranger into our private lives to change us?

The Kingdom of God grows. In the same way a seed grows, the Kingdom of God grows. In both cases God does the growing. When we are born again into the Kingdom of God, the Kingdom of God begins to grow in us. Science doesn't know how to create a seed that will grow into a plant. God does. In the same way, we are not able to grow the Kingdom of God within us. God does the growing. Our part is to agree with the process. When we cooperate and agree with him, the Holy Spirit will transform us from glory to glory into the image of Jesus. God rules in the Kingdom of God. Do we want him to rule in us?

We are living on a rebellious planet that is working against God's plan for his creation. The world is on a collision course with God's Kingdom. If we are living with our hearts divided between the two, we run the risk of being flattened during impact. If we don't want to become a casualty, we need to realize the Spirit of God is with us, hovering, the same way He hovered in the beginning when He hovered over the waters. And He's in us. He is growing us, as we agree with his plan for our lives. Wisdom says it would be a good idea for us to tune into what He is saying to us, to allow him to work through us. And as we become completely committed to him, He will then have complete sovereignty. Then God's rule will be growing in us. That means the authority of God will be growing in us and through us. And as we are dwelling in the Kingdom of God, He will be ruling over us, in us, and through us. That might be a problem for us? Would his rule be a challenge to our independence? A threat? We might think worshipping God is fine, but we are the ones who are in charge of our lives. We make the decisions.

We are sovereign. Wrong, if you have given your life to Jesus, that's exactly what it means. You have given your life to Jesus. He is the one who is your sovereign now, and you are to follow him. Is that a stumbling block maybe? No need to stumble. The good news is the good news. His rule is extremely gracious, kind, and loving. He is our Creator and He loves us. When we surrender our lives to him, then He has the freedom to live through us and with us.

But we might not be convinced. We might try to offer the excuse we can't hear him, so how can we obey him? Our excuse is meaningless because his instructions are all written down in his book. We have his book to read, and his Spirit is in us to give us insight. That is, if we do want to know him. And if we do decide He is the only way, then our hearts are revealed and vulnerable, ready for gentle correction as we are convicted of our actual state. Then we are given the choice of allowing him to change us, or not, to allow him to reign in our lives, or not. God the Father reigned in the life of Jesus. We know He did, because Jesus only did what he saw the Father doing. He was obedient to his Father. And He sacrificed himself for us. The healing and the miracles were a sign of the Kingdom of God coming. They were not the main event. The main event was his death and resurrection. Jesus didn't spend his life thinking, "Oh, man, this is cool, healing people, doing miracles, raising the dead, wow, I'm so in God's will." Those events were only a sign of the King and the Kingdom coming. But what if we were allowed to do the miraculous works of the Kingdom just as Jesus did? In our present state of immaturity we might become deluded and imagine ourselves ruling the universe. We might think it would be pretty cool, pretty powerful, to go around ruling and healing everyone, performing miracles, and whatever came to mind. Here's something to consider. If that's what we think our lives would be like, then God isn't ruling in our lives. When Jesus came He lived his life in opposition to self-glorification. He came to serve. Jesus was serving the Father and us. God's nature is sacrificial. He gives himself for others, and the Holy Spirit is also sacrificial. The Holy Spirit serves the Father and Jesus and us. The Holy Spirit is in us, healing us, comforting us, giving himself for us and for Jesus and for the Father. And we know the Father gave his only begotten Son for us. Jesus made it possible for us to live in his Kingdom, and He has sent the Holy Spirit to us to direct us in our lives. He helps us, guides us, and shows us things to come. The Holy Spirit teaches us, encourages us, tells us about Jesus, abides with us, and empowers us to be witnesses.

To grow we need to be hungry. How hungry are we for more of him?

CHAPTER THIRTY-FOUR

In my first job as a reporter I worked on a local, small-town newspaper. Yes, I was a reporter for a while. I even took journalism courses at university. Anyway, one requirement of my reporting job was taking pictures. When I started the job my experience using a camera was little to none. To resolve my predicament, I decided I'd try to make a deal with God. If He would take the pictures, I wouldn't take credit for them. As a result He took some incredible pictures, and I didn't take credit for them. Once in a while the editor would decide to give me a byline, but I never claimed credit for myself. At the time I didn't tell anyone, including the editor, about the deal I'd made. Besides, the editor would have balked at giving a picture credit that read, Photo by God.

God later discouraged me from making any more deals with Him. When I was considering returning to university to take my Master's Degree in English, I decided to throw out a fleece. Remember Gideon? If you don't know about fleeces and want to, read Gideon's story in the Book of Judges. Anyway, I had a wife and three young children at home, and I wasn't sure if this was the right time to go back to university. Also, to enable me to attend I needed to apply for a bursary. I asked God to give me a sign if He was in agreement with my proposal. The sign I presented to him was that my bursary would be approved. Later when the bursaries were listed, I discovered I had received even more than the amount I had applied for. I stood outside the university accounts office staring at my name on the list and the amount granted. Then I heard that still small voice say, "Now make a mature decision." I did. Even though I received more than I asked for, I knew this was not the time for me to go back to school. I realized the idea had only come from selfish me. And that was the last time I bothered God with a fleece, or tried to bargain with him.

Waiting isn't easy. Of course we know that our western culture does not major on waiting. The urgency of getting what we want is rampant in our society. We are being driven by forces in the world system, compelling us to become slaves to it. And there's no end in sight, unless we stop and decide to live in God's system. Love is what we really need, and love is free in the Kingdom of God. Love for God and for one another, it's free. In the Kingdom of God our basic needs are met. Our need for significance and security are met. We have gifts and talents He has graced us with so we can serve him and one another. We are secure and can find meaning when we are living in a community of believers. Then we are able to wait on him. We have nothing to prove. We have no Kingdom to build for ourselves, because we are already living in one, our Savior's. Seeing our lives from an eternal perspective, we can make the most of our time here. We might ask, what are we waiting for in the Kingdom of God? That's easy. We are waiting on God. We don't need to spend most of our time focusing on the world and how we are to serve the world's agenda, and on our own needs, and our wants. Instead, we can and discover his plan for us in the world and serve our King.

We have been saved from sin and death. That means we can live free from the anxiety and fear they bring. And we can live free of the fear of not measuring up to some human standard dictated by our culture. Or for those in church leadership, we can live free of the fear of not measuring up to some ideal model of ministry. True wisdom is to wait on the Lord to make our decisions. Christians often say they don't have their prayers answered. Or they say they are not receiving an answer from God concerning what they are supposed to do in certain, important situations. We might ask in response to that complaint, have you been communicating with God every day, or only when you need something, and you want an answer? If you have been talking to him, if you have been developing a deeper relationship with him, you will be happy even if He isn't giving you an immediate answer to your prayer. He might be delaying his answer to see if you will seek him even more. He might be encouraging you to make a habit of talking to him more frequently. He really loves that. He really loves his children talking to him.

So how is your waiting coming along? And what are you waiting for? If you are living in the Kingdom of God, then first and foremost you are waiting like the rest of us for Jesus to come back. And while we are waiting, we are fulfilling the great commission to see people set free and become disciples of Jesus. In other words, we are also on a mission. The trouble is we have a habit of accepting the mission and then trying to accomplish it our way, without waiting to listen, without waiting for our listening ability and our character to develop. We might decide to develop our own methods, patterned after the world's way of doing things, or maybe we might become discouraged and give up entirely. In our immaturity we often insert our wants and desires into God's plan for our lives and call those wants and desires his plan. Of course, God blesses some of our additions to his plan for us. And sometimes our desires coincide with his plan for us. They are desires He has put there. But then often we run ahead, like children, to see them fulfilled immediately. We need to be patient and listen to the Holy Spirit's plan for our lives. We need to wait and take the time. We need to be aware that his ways are not our ways.

We are not able to live in the world and accomplish the mission we have each been given in our spheres of influence, unless we have developed the ability to hear what the Holy Spirit is saying to us in any given situation. For instance, we might think it is imperative to witness to our colleagues at work or our classmates at school in ways that are intrusive and not inspired by God, and then as a result cause more harm than good. But when we first wait to hear what God is saying, then our effectiveness in being witnesses to the lost will increase and our relationship with our Father in Heaven will also deepen, which is an end in itself.

We might not hear every day the specific things we are to do, but at least we will be developing the routine of first praying and reading scripture and trying to hear what He is saying to us. After a while living in the Spirit will become like the way our autonomic nervous system functions. We don't have to tell our heart to beat or our stomach to digest. We need to get into the habit of being aware of his presence, hearing his voice when He is speaking, being at peace, and waiting for any Kingdom instructions He might have for us.

CHAPTER THIRTY-FIVE

My first church I told you about, the one with the Freedom Center outreach, held a baptism ceremony at a local lake one Sunday afternoon. A family of four was being baptized. The baptizers and the candidates were standing in the water waste deep. The afternoon sun's rays sparkled on the water, as the Spirit of God hovered over the joyful group of six. I was sitting on the grassy shore taking in the spiritual event, when I noticed there were suddenly only five. One of the baptizers had disappeared beneath the glistening lake. Unusual, I thought, but there was no need to panic. And then a hand appeared above the water coming toward shore, and then a gasping head popped up, and then the head and hand disappeared below the surface again. No need to panic, I thought. A few seconds later, the hand and gasping head reappeared, coming ever closer to shore. No need to help, I thought. The Spirit of God was in control. Others on the shore who were witnessing the event seemed content to let the drowning play out. Up and sputtering, he came again, this time crawling till he reached the shore, exhausted. I sat beside him, as he lay there. He was bewildered but peaceful, and still alive, a cloud of God's peace surrounding us. He didn't tell me what business God had been doing with him as he was drowning in the Spirit. But a few years later, in middle-age, he emi-grated to Australia and became an Anglican Priest.

The supernatural peace of God is to be found in the Kingdom of God. We have been given the opportunity to experience the supernatural peace of God when we are living in his supernatural Kingdom. I believe right now today the Spirit of God is emphasizing our need to live in his Kingdom-of-God peace, his supernatural peace.

We know of course peace isn't just the absence of war, although most people in the world generally see it that way. The lie has been peddled that if we would only stop fighting one another and learn how to get along, then we would have world peace. The ultimate source of that lie is the Devil. World peace is not ever going to be realized, given the fallen state of human beings. Besides, real, genuine peace goes much deeper than the absence of war. Real peace is a supernatural state of being. The Kingdom of God is supernatural, and, of course, the world is in the natural realm. The world will never know peace until the Prince of Peace returns to rule.

Have you ever worried about something to the point where you're frantic? In 1995, I was at that con-ference in Toronto I already told you about, and I couldn't get through to my wife and kids back home. There was no nation-wide calling in those days, so I had to rely on pay phones, or the phone in the hotel room. No matter what I did, I couldn't get through. I was worried. The phone would ring and ring but no one would answer. This continued for several days.

Had something happened? I knew, of course, that if there had been something wrong at home my wife would have called my hotel and left a message. But there was no message, and I couldn't get through, either.

During the conference an instruction was given by one of the speakers that we ask the Lord if there were any issues in our lives we needed to address. I asked. In answer to my question, the still small voice said one word, "Worry." Worrying is hard to stop. But I'm sure you know that. And you guessed it. There was no emergency at home. I had created the emergency in my mind. And 26-years later I'm still trying to stop worrying. I know the remedy, too. I know the scripture. In fact, I often recite the verses to others who are anxious or fearful. Here they are.

"Be anxious for nothing, but in everything by prayer and supplication, with thanksgiving, let your requests be made known to God; and the peace of God, which surpasses all understanding, will guard your hearts and minds through Christ Jesus.." Philippians 4:6-7

Let's consider for a moment who this is who is trying to tell us something. Paul the apostle is writing those words. But the words he is writing are a message coming directly from God. Jesus is the word of God. But the words on the paper aren't him. The essence of their meaning, what the words are telling us, is him. The words are Jesus communicating to us. When we are reading his word, we are reading him and internalizing who He is into our lives. We are taking his truth into ourselves, and then He changes us when, in the power of his Holy Spirit, we agree with his word, which means we are agreeing with him. That means we need to be continually getting to know him and reading his word, so that we will know when He is the one who is speaking to us. We need to receive the perspective of the one who saved us. His perspective is a Kingdom of God perspective. We ought to be living in the light of his truth. The Holy Spirit, of course, knows the truth. The Holy Spirit is the Truth; He is the Spirit of Truth. The apostle Paul knows the truth, too.

Wisdom would tell us it would be wise at least to consider what Paul is writing to us, since God is the one speaking to us. We might also like to consider the trials Paul endured in his lifetime. During his God-given mission to take the Gospel to the Gentiles, he was beaten to a pulp and lived in constant peril. He is the one agreeing with God and telling us we are to be anxious for nothing. We also need to remember that at one point in his journey he was taken into the third heaven and saw life from God's perspective, a heavenly perspective. The one who lived in constant danger and was eventually martyred, and who also saw life from God's perspective, is telling us we can live in the peace of God. That means the peace of God is available in this life for us to live in, or he wouldn't be telling us we can. Paul is telling us this, but he is not the only one sharing with us this valuable information. The heart of God is also telling us this.

So let's take a closer look at this message from God

to help us understand the truth He is communicating to us. In the process, the hope is that we would be changed. The hope is that our hearts would be changed and come into agreement with God's heart. I'm still trying to agree with him and be changed.

"Be anxious for nothing, but in everything by prayer and supplication, with thanksgiving, let your requests be made known to God." The word in the Greek translated "anxious" means to be troubled with cares. If you have never been troubled with cares, you might want to stop reading now. But I think most of us at one time or another have been troubled with cares. Maybe some of us are constantly being troubled with cares. Although, in our minds we might know being troubled with cares, no matter how genuine we might think they are, can be a big waste of time and energy. But we often do it anyway. We might even indulge our anxiety. We might even find wallowing in despair is somewhat enjoyable. We might even indulge ourselves by falling into a pool of bitter-sweet, pleasurable melancholy? Dear me, what will become of us all?

There is a remedy to being anxious, if we want one. The remedy seems to be the hard part. The scripture is written in the form of a command. We are told to be anxious for nothing. The word "nothing" is translated from the Greek, and it means nothing. The Holy Spirit of God is telling us through the apostle Paul, to be anxious for nothing. Don't be troubled with cares. Stop doing that. But our response might be that stopping is hard to do. In fact, how in the world are we going to stop? We are next given an answer to that question. Instead of being anxious we are told to do something else instead. Paul tells us to replace our anxiety by taking action, and the action isn't to run off in all directions, doing something. It is an action we can all take. Here it is: "But in everything by prayer and supplication, with thanksgiving, let your requests be made known to God." Instead of dwelling on our troubles and cares, we are told to talk to our Father in heaven about them. But we know, of course, He is too busy most of the time with more pressing demands, and He isn't required to listen to our petty problems. We can only talk to him about the really important things. Is that what Paul tells us? No, that's not what the word of God says. The Holy Spirit is telling us we can talk to him about "everything." No matter what it is, instead of suffering in our anxiety, we are told to bring our concerns to God and earnestly ask him to take care of whatever it is. And then leave it there with him, especially those things we are helpless to do anything about ourselves. And we repeat the request if necessary, and continue to repeat it, if necessary. Of course, the more desperate we believe our situation to be, the more earnest and urgent our requests will be. But as a bonus, in the process of talking to him, we will get to know him better.

Now let's notice the words "with thanksgiving" inserted in there. Paul tells us we are to live in a state of thanksgiving, as we make our requests known to God. After all, we believers in Christ have been saved, which is really something to be thankful for. We thank our Father for who He is and for what Jesus Christ has done for us. We thank God for all of our circumstances, no matter what they are, in everything, because of what He has done for us. We are here, we are alive, and we are saved for eternity. We might not always be enjoying what is going on in our lives in the world out there, but at the same time, our relationship with our Father in Heaven and our eternal destiny are being established in the Kingdom of God. I think we would all agree we usually remember to thank God for all the blessings He has given us. But what about those experiences in our lives that are disagreeable and unpleasant. Do we thank him for those, the ones that come from the world out there? What about those? There must be a reason they come along.

In fact, I don't think anyone has, or can, escape them. We spend our lives trying to escape the trials, but Christians and non-Christians alike will all experience challenges. And those challenges help us to grow, or not. So are we thankful for those trying times in our lives, the ones that give us an opportunity to grow? When believers are interacting with the world, there is a clash of kingdoms. And those clashes can cause growth in character. We need to thank him for the refining that comes when we face challenges in our lives. Are we able to see our challenges from his perspective, a Kingdom of God perspective? Then there are those minor daily challenges. They might seem insignificant, but they help us to grow in character. For instance, responding with a soft answer to a spouse, when he or she pushes our entrenched anger button. We know, of course, we can have bigger challenges in our daily lives than marital spats. But what about what Jesus had to face? We haven't had to face challenges that enormous, to take on the sins of the world. But this is what He said on the Cross about the ultimate challenge, "Father, forgive them, for they do not know what they are doing." He also tells us to, "love your enemies, bless those who curse you, do good to those who hate you, and pray for those who spitefully use you and persecute you." Matthew 5:44

Most of us have seldom, if ever, had to face major challenges, such as being reviled and persecuted. Then again, we don't know what the future might hold. If it happens that we do have to face severe kinds of challenges in the future, how are we going to respond? Right now we have the choice of agreeing with Jesus, or not agreeing, to be in training for what lies ahead, or not. Jesus says we are blessed, when we endure persecution and false accusation. Will we be able to live in a state of thanksgiving when we are badly treated? God really wants us to grow up in him. Are we willing to thank God for the process of growing us up? Are we thankful for the trials? Are we able to thank him for maturing us so we can grow into becoming like him, so we can know him in a deeper way, and to become Christ-like, and to be joint-heirs with him, loved equally by our Father in heaven?

Next we read "the peace of God, which surpasses all understanding, will guard our hearts and minds through Christ Jesus." How does that work, and what is this peace all about? According to Strong's Concordance the Greek word here translated "peace" means "the tranquil state of a soul assured of its salvation through Christ, and so the soul fearing nothing from God is content with its earthly lot, of whatsoever sort that is." Now how is that possible? It sounds like the ideal all right, but it also sounds impossible. And not too exciting. To be content with our earthly lot? How do we become content? If we are going to eliminate anxiety and live in such a tranquil state, there must be something more to this whole concept of peace. But when we read further, we discover there is a lot more to this word "peace." This kind of peace is the kind that "surpasses all understanding." Well, we still might ask, what kind of peace is that? Or might those words be written there simply as a way to fill out the sentence neatly? What does "surpasses all understanding" mean? The answer to the question is simple. It means we can't understand it. How's that for a brilliant answer? Since it is far beyond our ability to understand, and if it's the peace of God, which means it comes from God, then it follows that this kind of peace must be entirely supernatural. It must be a Kingdom of God kind of peace. And this kind of peace will guard our hearts and our minds through Christ Jesus. So Jesus has made this kind of peace available. He is the Prince of Peace. He has brought his peace into the world even though the world rejected him. But for those who put their trust in him, the supernatural peace of God is available for us to live in. We are even invited to live there. But how do we live there? It must be hard to live there, since we all know that on most days there is a lot going on around us. And, after all, we have to get through our day. With all the things we have to focus on, and with all the distractions, how can we live in his peace? The answer is somehow we have to take our lives to God, and we have to live our lives in him. Then the supernatural peace of God will come upon us, and our minds will be put at rest. Then the noise and cares of this world are heard and seen but not allowed to dominate our lives. The peace of God will prevail, because we will have another perspective, God's eternal perspective. Instead of the turmoil coming at us and disturbing us, and causing anxiety, the peace of God will go out from us, causing a change in the spiritual atmosphere around us. Then those around us might begin to notice. But what they notice won't be us. They will be sensing the supernatural presence of the peace of God.

God is not anxious. He's not worried. He knows the end from the beginning. His Kingdom, the Kingdom of God, is peace. The Kingdom of God is at hand. When we are living in him, He guards us, and He silences the noise coming from outside, and He silences the inner noise stirring in our minds. When we are living in his peace, the things of this world come into right perspective, his perspective, a Kingdom of God perspective. And his peace will transform us. When our minds begin to be transformed, we will begin to have a deeper understanding of God's will for our lives and the truth of his Word will go deeper into our hearts.

Even though the world in this age is passing away, the world system still wants us to be completely committed to it, to be fully occupied with it, until we are totally consumed by it. But God says his plan is for us to be transformed. Believers in Christ are a new creation in him.

So according to God's Word, what are we to do? When we are anxious, first we take our cares to our Father in heaven, thankful we can talk to him and know we are his for eternity, and then we leave our cares with him. Next we see that the peace of God, which we cannot understand, guards our hearts and minds from inner and outer turmoil, and in the process our minds are transformed by being renewed, and our old way of living in, and being consumed by, the cares of this world are replaced by the mind of Christ. We then begin to see the world and our lives here on earth from his viewpoint. And in the supernatural peace of God we are able to hear what He is saying to us. And we begin to understand more and more the truth of scripture. And we begin to hear more clearly what the Holy Spirit is saying to us about our lives and what our purpose is here in this life, so we begin to live in his perfect will for us. And our minds are set free from the anxiety the world tries to impose upon us. And those obstacles that keep us seeing only from an earthly viewpoint will increasingly be removed from our lives.

There's no anxiety in a safe place, and we have been offered a safe place of supernatural peace in which to live. Jesus brings peace into the world for those who want peace. We know his peace will ultimately prevail. We have a lot to be thankful for. And those steadfast believers who have been poor in this life will have everything when they go to be with him. And when bad things do happen in our lives, we are to continue to be anxious for nothing and continue to live in him, and in his peace. There is a lot of anxiety in the world today, and it is increasing on a global scale. And there isn't any current sign that life in the world will become any less stressful. But Jesus has called us out of this world and into his Kingdom, which is the only safe place to be, now and for eternity.

CHAPTER THIRTY-SIX

In 2000, the year of the Y2K non-event, a few of us went to a conference in Albany, Oregon. Bob Jones was one of the speakers. Following the preaching, Jones gave prophetic words to those who had lined up. I was questioning at the time about continuing in ministry. The prophetic word I got from Bob, and the Holy Spirit, was not to resign, but to re-sign. Since then, I've now re-signed for another twenty years, and counting.

As I was thinking about notable spiritual events in my life, I was reminded of many more that were significant. In case you were wondering, this writing wasn't intended to be my swan song but a primer for the future. I'm eager to see all the great and wonderful things God is going to do on this earth before He returns. And He is going to accomplish many of them through us, his "ekklesia," his called out ones. So I'm looking forward to what He is going to do next. But at the same time, I am most thankful for the deepening communion I am having with him, which far outweighs anything I might do in this life, including raising the dead or telling mountains to move. As a notable, contemporary prophet once said, "raising the dead, or taking a nap, the pay's the same."

In 2013, I was flying to a conference in New Jersey. We were flying over Arizona to land in Phoenix, where I would make my east coast connection. My mind was speeding and worrying about just about anything and everything I could think of, including family, church, and whatever. And why was I going to this conference anyway? My mind was speeding along, listing all the things I needed to be concerned about, including being 30,000 feet in the air. And then I heard it. I heard that still small voice. The still small voice said, "I'll walk you home." Panic was my immediate response. The plane was going to crash, and I was going to die. But then the image of Jesus walking me home calmed my mind, and then his peace settled on me.

Of course, Jesus was walking me home. Then all the worries my speeding mind was reviewing dissolved in the peace of his presence. I understood. We would be walking home, and we might stop here or there, or go and talk to those people over there, or do whatever might come along on my journey home with Jesus. He is walking all of us home, those of us who are born-again into His Kingdom. It's wonderful to know we are all out for a Kingdom walk, and we can walk right on through into eternity without a break in the action. It's been done before. We know Enoch took the trip. "All the days of Enoch were three hundred and sixty-five years. And Enoch walked with God; and he was not, for God took him." Genesis 5:23. That's a long walk, a record breaking one, and Enoch didn't even have a Fitbit.

So I did make it to that conference in New Jersey.

Rick Joyner, Larry Randolph, Ray Hughes, and Dennis Cramer were there. Cramer called me out of the congregation, which had never happened to me before, and the highlight of the prophetic word he gave to me was, "Like Father, like son."

At the same conference, prophetic minister Larry Randolph gave a message that stood out in my mind. His message included a vision of the future that likened the increasing presence of God in the earth to a dark room where a candle is lit. The room becomes increasingly brighter, as the candle becomes brighter and brighter. It wasn't a vision of revival but of progressive brightening in a dark world. I want to stay around to see how bright the light is going to get. We read in Habakkuk 2:14, "For the earth will be filled with the knowledge of the glory of the Lord as the waters cover the sea." The glory in this passage is that word "kavod" again. And that's a lot of kavod. So my hope is not just for revival. And although periodic bursts of increased light from the candle will be wonderful events, we need to persevere to see a permanent and increasing Kingdom of God presence that will bring an ever-increasing revelation of the heart of Jesus and what our purpose and function is for the times we are living in. And our purpose includes, of course, being instrumental in seeing many come into God's Kingdom. In his presence, in his glory, salvation and the love of God are found. God's presence changes us, as we give our lives to Jesus, and as we follow him, becoming his true disciples.

We need to persevere. But the trials and obstacles

can cause us to feel like quitting. Have you ever begun to think this Christian journey is just too much? The opposition is too fierce? Maybe there are members of your family who are part of the resistance. They simply don't get it, and they seem to become hostile for no apparent reason. Representing the King can make for a challenging life. But the reward for persevering can be immeasurable. We are in enemy territory, and there are demonic forces at work defending their territory. People's hearts are the territory, so quitting isn't really an option.

The reward for persevering is the harvest of souls. The Baby Boomers need to persevere and sign up for God's program, not retire. Even as Caleb and the Joshua in the Old Testament persevered to enter their Promised Land, we also need to persevere and go into our Promised Land. We need to be standing in the truth, so we can pass a legacy on to the next generation. But first our generation needs to be saved, and those of us who have been saved and have been in the battle for a long time, we need to ask God to reinvigorate us, to reignite the fire in us, so we can carry on in the battle.

If you have been in the battle for many years, you know we can get worn out. We can get tired of the whole thing, can't we? But we can find some encouragement in Hebrews 6:10, "For God is not unjust to forget your work and labor of love which you have shown toward His name, in that you have ministered to the saints, and do minister. And we desire that each one of you show the same diligence to the full assurance of hope until the end, that you do not become sluggish, but imitate those who through faith and patience inherit the promises."

Now I can see myself back there again, on the Jordan River bank, where I was sitting in November, 2017, when I was 70 years old, and when Israel was approaching its 70th birthday. I'm a few years older now, by the time you read this. But there I am sitting in perfect peace in Israel, a born-again believer for forty years, having just been dramatically affirmed by my Father in heaven. And now I'm continuing to go forward, onward and upward to finish well. Not that I'm expecting to finish anytime soon. Age doesn't matter much. Moses left the planet at the age of 120. That's still on the books.

Being the pastor of a church dedicated to following Jesus isn't easy. Resistance can be formidable, but without resistance there isn't any growth, and spiritual muscles can atrophy. Living as a Christian couch potato is no way to live. This is no time in history to shrink back from the battle. Jesus didn't die for us to live in fear. Onward and upward is the only way to go.

So if you have the idea you might want to quit, forget it. You can make it all the way through to the end and finish well. And if you haven't heard, here's some great news for you. God's body on earth, the Church, the "ekklesia," is coming awake in North America and in various other parts of the world, and the supernatural is going to become normal for those who are committed to go the distance with Jesus and embrace the crucified life. That's all to come. And I know I'm going to live as long as He wants me to live.

There is nothing I have, or am, that God hasn't given me. He created me. I am His. Gifts, talents, abilities, all have been given to me by him. My contribution has been to persevere and endure the pain.

An image came to my mind a few years ago. I was looking down on the earth from space. The earth was dark and had seams, as you would see on a soccer ball, but they were not symmetrical. The seams looked like fragile, bright, electric filaments connected by nodes in various places. My understanding was that the nodes were apostolic/prophetic church resource centers. And these words came to my mind when I saw this image, "My company is arising all over the earth. Come forth and lay a foundation for many generations." That statement at the time was contrary to my view of end time events, but then again we don't know when Jesus will return and when this age will end. So here is some encouragement for you: Despite the darkness trying to flood the earth and what seems like a declining Church in our part of the world, his true spiritual body is becoming more and more alive.

If you haven't caught it by now, here's my message to you: yes, you can make it. And the rewards for enduring to the end are impossible for us living here on earth to imagine. God will bring you through, if you let Him. I know. He has brought me through. I intend to finish well, but not for a while yet. I'm just getting started, how about you?

So I will end my story where I started, remembering my Jordan River baptism. At the hotel that night my mind wanted to make some sense of what had happened in the Jordan that day. You might have wondered what it was all about, too. So I decided to ask Him.

"Why?" was my basic question and, "What was that all about?"

"You were already baptized once, weren't you?" the still small voice said.

"Yes, "I said. "But..."

"But it was fun, wasn't it?" He said.

"Yes," I said, "it was fun."

The End

BOOKS BY THIS AUTHOR

The Dregs Of Aquarius

Fresh, insightful, and often hilarious, The Dregs of Aquarius is a counter-culture Catcher in the Rye that speaks to the generation coming of age now, as well as to those Baby Boomers who can't remember much about the whole scene and might want a refresher. And for those who might simply want to get away to another time and place that is authentically portrayed, The Dregs of Aquarius is the perfect trip.

The Darkest Valley

In the Cowichan Valley on beautiful Vancouver Island, a pastor's wife with a deep secret is dying of cancer, his young aboriginal convert is in danger of being grabbed and initiated into brutal Longhouse spirit dancing rituals, and his congregation is throwing him to the wolves. In desperation, he attempts to recruit a local newspaper editor to publish the truth about the Longhouse. Along the way truth is put to the test, and when his wife's secret is revealed, so is their faith.

The Good Book Club

PI Jane Sunday investigates the murder of the associate pastor of a church gone wrong. A solid jolt of detective fiction, The Good Book Club compels lovers of the genre to hold on tight to the emotional rollercoaster until the very end.

My Fear Lady

Gumshoe Joe LaFlam again goes head-to-head with Spelunkers Global, this time going undercover undground to bust the conspirators. And also get the girl.

Bye Bye Bertie

Investigating a kidnapping case, gumshoe Joe LaFlam runs afoul of Spelunkers Global, a secret society bent on world domination. Joe undertakes a desperate 21-day fast to twist God's arm to help him solve the case, make some good money, and get the girl, any girl.